LogicalCHOICE
Facilitator's Guide

LogicalCHOICE Facilitator's Guide

Welcome and Introduction... 3

You Have Choices..4

Case Study: The Connected Classroom..............................5

Making the Transition to the Connected Classroom.............9

Configuring the Learning Environment...............................10

The LogicalCHOICE Experience...18

Delivering a LogicalCHOICE Course...................................21

Presentation Best Practices..24

Conclusion: Making the Transition to Virtual 28

Welcome and Introduction

Time and distance are no longer the barriers to delivering training that they once were. Social networks, collaboration tools, and videoconferencing technologies enable you to overcome such barriers, so you can deliver training that meets the needs of learners, facilitators, and your organization. However, teaching in an environment that uses these technologies provides new challenges and requires that facilitators and learners get accustomed to new ways of interacting.

The Logical Operations LogicalCHOICE product line recognizes these new challenges and provides support for teaching and learning in such an environment as well as in the traditional classroom. This guide will take a look at special considerations of teaching in the twenty-first century classroom. It will introduce to the LogicalCHOICE product and provide guidelines to help you successfully deliver courses in the new paradigm.

You Have Choices

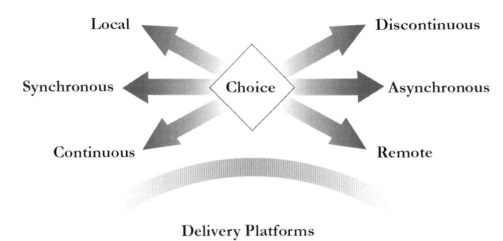

Delivery Platforms

Figure 1: Choice across multiple dimensions of delivery

When you plan a collaborative learning experience, you make decisions along various dimensions that define the collaborative learning experience. With today's conferencing and collaboration technologies, you have more options than ever before in regard to the logistics of delivery, including:

- **Presence** *(local versus remote)*: Learners may be present within the same classroom, or they may be virtual—connected through videoconferencing technologies such as teleconferencing, messaging, and computer desktop sharing.

- **Synchronicity** *(synchronous versus asynchronous)*: Learners may work through the course at the same time, or they may work through parts of the course on their own, at different times.

- **Continuity** *(continuous versus discontinuous)*: Learning may occur over a single span, such as an eight-hour training day. Or it may occur in installments over multiple periods of time.

- **Delivery Platforms:** An array of technologies is available to support the delivery of training across the other dimensions of learning.

You may need to cover a combination of these dimensions. For example, while you may have some learners present in the classroom, you may have others simultaneously connect to the classroom through videoconferencing technologies. They interact with you and other learners through audio and video connections provided through videoconferencing tools.

Case Study: The Connected Classroom

Twelve students have just settled in for a hands-on introductory course on Microsoft® Excel®. At first glance, the classroom looks like any other. Students are seated at computer workstations with Excel displayed on their screens. Each student has a training manual. The instructor writes on a whiteboard and discusses points highlighted on a Microsoft® PowerPoint® slide. But something is different about this classroom. It's a LogicalCHOICE classroom.

Figure 2: LogicalCHOICE facilitator workstation and classroom layout

Students Can Choose a Location

Seven of the 12 students are present and seated in the classroom, but five students aren't physically present in the classroom at all. They're in remote locations, accessing the classroom through video-conferencing tools. In the classroom, a video feed of each student is displayed on one of the large monitors mounted on the classroom wall, with each student's name displayed above his or her video feed. Some of the remote students, it seems, are seated at kitchen tables or in home offices. Another student is in an office cubicle setting and is wearing a headset so his audio feed doesn't disturb his cubicle neighbors. Some students have print manuals, and others are viewing their manuals on ebook readers and tablets.

The Instructor Interacts with Local and Remote Learners

The classroom is extended through the connections to the outside world. The technology, course materials, and interactions are designed so the instructor can interact with local and remote learners on an equal basis.

The classroom is arranged so the facilitator can see students' computer screens and move freely about the room. At times the instructor teaches from the whiteboard. Other times, the instructor teaches from her workstation near the back of the room.

The instructor—let's call her the *course facilitator*—actually has several monitors attached to her presentation computer. One is the monitor that displays the student video feeds in the classroom.

Another monitor is displayed through an interactive display in front of the room. The facilitator touches the screen to interact with it as though using a mouse on a giant computer monitor. The facilitator highlights and marks up portions of the screen so that all students, local and remote, can see the markup. This is what she uses for most of her presentations.

The facilitator can also use the interactive display through a special wireless tablet and pen, which she carries with her as she moves throughout the room. Sometimes she works directly at the interactive whiteboard. Other times, she presents from her workstation. Because she has complete control from any location, she isn't bound to the front of the room or to a facilitator station. She can freely move about the room and interact with both her local and remote learners. She wears a wireless microphone so her voice is always audible.

One monitor at the facilitator's workstation is set up for her private viewing. She uses this monitor for private side chats with learners to monitor their progress and to answer questions. From this monitor, she also views and retrieves her teaching notes, and opens files and launches presentations and external resources that she will incorporate into the course.

Remote and Local Students Interact With Each Other

LogicalCHOICE courses are designed to promote activity and collaboration among learners, regardless of learner location. In our example class, remote students have web cams mounted on their monitors, which give them a visual presence in the class. And learners in the local classroom are logged in to the same web conferencing tools that are being used by the remote learners, even though they are on-site. This levels the playing field, enabling on-site learners to interact with the remote learners through collaboration tools such as online messaging and polling tools. There are two additional cameras in the room, which the facilitator can use as needed to provide remote learners with a wide view of activities in the classroom.

When the class began, the facilitator zoomed up each student's video feed in turn, as students introduced themselves to the class and shared their expectations for the course. The facilitator's role in this environment is much expanded over that of *instructor*. The facilitator is constantly aware of *delivery* – attending to logistical details that influence the learning experience for both local and remote students. She adjusts the online presentation as needed to create the best possible experience. That includes making sure all students have an opportunity to see what they need to see, hear what they need to hear, say what they need to say, and do what they need to do.

The Facilitator Fosters a Productive Learning Environment

As the facilitator leads students through course activities, the local and remote students follow along in their LogicalCHOICE course manuals. Some students have chosen to use the tablet or e-book version of the manual. Others have chosen to use a print version.

As in the traditional local classroom, the facilitator promotes *interaction*, helps students to stay *engaged*, and *monitors* learners' progress, making course adjustments as needed. However, some of this must now be done in a mixed environment or from a distance. As in the traditional classroom, some training organizations may choose to split this responsibility among co-instructors. Or depending on class size and available resources, they may provide technical resources and support to enable one facilitator to handle it all.

When you're teaching across a distance, monitoring learner progress can be a challenge. For example, when the facilitator presents a new topic, she may begin with slides that introduce underlying concepts and principles. She then demonstrates the concept and associated procedures within the software application. Up to this point, there may be questions and dialogue, which are conducted through audio/video feeds supported by a web conferencing application. She might even use integrated polling and questioning tools to deliver a "pop quiz" to see if students are grasping the new material.

To attend to learner progress, when the facilitator releases learners to perform the activity on their own, she asks learners to click a button in the web conferencing tool to indicate when they have completed the activity, and she asks them to send her a private chat message if they are stuck or have any questions.

Learners Need Support in Hands-on Activities

One student has a question about something odd happening on his computer as he performs the activity. He shares his screen with her privately. The facilitator figures out the problem, but thinks it might actually provide an interesting learning opportunity for the entire class. She asks the student if he minds if she shares his screen with the whole class. He approves, so he shares his screen, and the facilitator guides the class through a troubleshooting exercise. Together they come up with the solution, and everyone learns from the experience.

Challenges and Opportunities of the Connected Classroom

In summary, training delivery is complicated enough. Add to that the complexity of teaching from a distance, and it's clear that the facilitator has a lot to tend to, including challenges such as:

- Communicating effectively.

- Promoting collaboration and interaction among participants.

- Fostering engagement.

- Monitoring learner performance; adjusting pacing and delivery as needed.

- Juggling among many concerns: content delivery, technology, learners with different needs, training logistics, and so forth.

However, with these challenges come new opportunities to extend the reach of your training, engage users in new ways, and incorporate new technology and new learning components to re-invent the traditional classroom learning experience. Let's see how you can make the transition to LogicalCHOICE.

Making the Transition to the Connected Classroom

As you start implementing training across the dimensions of delivery, you will find that your old definitions and ways of doing things start to change. The words *instructor*, *teacher*, and *trainer* may no longer adequately describe the role of the course leader. You may also find that you no longer need an instructor station at the front of the room; in fact, with such a connected classroom, the person who leads the course could be located *anywhere*—even offsite.

The role of instructor in the new paradigm tends to be far more than one who instructs. In the connected classroom, the course leader not only *delivers instruction* but plays the more comprehensive role of *facilitating learning*. An expert facilitator is adept at not only delivering instruction, but in facilitating the types of activities in which students learn together.

Conversely, students play a more active role than simply receiving the lecture. The design of the connected classroom helps to create an effective environment for collaboration and learning.

LogicalCHOICE training materials have been designed to support you in making the transition. They are designed with features to help you be more effective in a connected classroom as well as in the traditional classroom.

The following sections provide you with guidelines to successfully make the transition to a Logical-CHOICE classroom, including setting up the facilitator and student environments, using training materials, and facilitation best practices.

Configuring the Learning Environment

There are many ways to configure your connected classroom. The precise configuration you use will be determined by various factors, including budget, space, availability of hardware and resources, and the needs of your learners and other training stakeholders. As a model, here is a list of the major components you'll typically want to incorporate into your LogicalCHOICE virtual classroom.

Facilitator Environment Design

A good design for the facilitator's working environment is the starting point for a successful Logical CHOICE course experience.

Figure 3: LogicalCHOICE facilitator workstation and classroom layout

Facilitator's workstation: This will serve several functions. It is the command, communication, and control center for the training event. This is where you will coordinate and guide the learning event. It is also the primary broadcast and communication hub for the classroom, hosts the web conference software, and is also configured with the demo applications, slides, and other media that you'll broadcast to the participants during the session. Look for a robust, reliable, versatile PC with plenty of memory, storage capacity, and flexible and powerful graphics support.

Internet: Well-connected, reliable, fast Internet connectivity is a must.

Web sharing software: Selecting and mastering your websharing tool is second in importance only to your mastery of the course content itself. See the "Enabling Technologies" section for some of the features and capabilities you may want to consider when you standardize on this key tool.

Video: You'll need appropriately-placed web cams so virtual students can see the facilitator and other aspects of the classroom, and so the facilitator is able to move away from the workstation as needed.

Displays: Plan for multiple displays; one for the facilitator's own desktop (which will also be projected in the classroom and shared in the web meeting); a large monitor to display the video feeds of all participants, giving them a visual presence in the classroom, and potentially a private monitor for housekeeping tasks and for private communications. For example, there may be times when learners do not want to have their questions to the instructor made public, so they can post private chat messages here. You can also use the private monitor to review teaching notes, launch presentation files, and so forth.

Interactive whiteboard: In the classroom, an interactive whiteboard can be a great tool for the instructor to focus learner attention by performing markup or highlighting important screen features. Remote students will need a video feed on the board; or you may choose to rely entirely on the whiteboarding features of your web sharing application.

Audio: You'll need an audio solution. You can use microphones and speakers, or opt for phone communications. If you use a mic and speakers, a wireless microphone is a great tool for maintaining the audio portion of the web broadcast from anywhere in the room. You may need additional microphones for the student areas, as well as speakers placed so everyone can hear virtual students when they contribute.

Figure 4: Facilitator screen layout

Student Environment Design

Figure 5: LogicalCHOICE student work areas—local and remote

The LogicalCHOICE student environment includes:

- Access to the software environment used to key the course, when appropriate. This may be a classroom computer, a locally-configured computer for remote students, or access to a virtual lab environment.

- Client access to the web-sharing software. This may involve installing a small client component on the student's local computer, or it may be purely a browser-based solution.

- A web-connected computer with a web cam. Remote students should have personal webcams if possible; on-site students may have individual cameras as well, or there may be general classroom cameras.

- Microphone or telephone headset/speakerphone, depending on whether audio will be provided through the web conferencing software or through the telephone. Remote students working from an office cubicle environment may find a headset necessary to avoid disturbing cubicle neighbors. On site, the audio can be configured through classroom microphones and speakers or the telephone.

  In general, the audio/video link should be designed so that remote and on-site learners can all see and interact with each other as smoothly as possible.

Figure 6: Example of a student screen layout

The student screen layout should be arranged to minimize the need for switching between windows. In the best possible configuration, students have a large monitor (or multiple monitors in an extended desktop) and can arrange everything (web conferencing windows, local instance of applications they are working with in practice activities, and student manual ebook) with minimal overlap of windows, so they can work without having to switch between windows.

Enabling Technologies

A wide variety of technologies are available to support the classroom of choice.

Web Conferencing Software

Web conferencing software provides a delivery platform for distance learning and collaboration, including many of the tools you need to provide instructor-led training from a distance. Example web conferencing platforms include iLinc, Cisco WebEx, Citrix GoToMeeting, Microsoft Lync, Adobe Connect, and numerous others.

Features that are commonly found in web conferencing technologies include the following.

Computer desktop sharing	The ability to broadcast the display of a computer desktop is obviously useful for delivering hands-on computer training demos. But other subject matter may be delivered successfully this way as well. Screen sharing enables you to broadcast to a learner audience many of those things that you can display on a computer, including slides, graphics, and documents. But some materials, such as videos and animations, may not transmit particularly well in this manner. You may find you need to use other means to broadcast such media. If your system supports it, learners can share their screens with you, enabling you to provide remote support and help as learners perform activities on their own computers.
Remote control	If desktop sharing includes the ability for a remote user to use their own mouse and keyboard to control the shared computer, then you have *remote control* capability. This opens up numerous possibilities, such as giving learners practice time on remote systems that they might not normally be able to access on their own.
Slide display	PowerPoint and other presentation programs can be used in conjunction with desktop sharing to present slides. Some presentation tools provide a special environment for PowerPoint slide display, including options to highlight and mark up slides, as well as share slide sets with learners after the presentation.
Shared whiteboard	By typing or drawing on a whiteboard application, presentation window, or shared application window, meeting participants can add drawings or annotations that can be viewed by all.
File sharing	File-sharing features provided by many web conferencing applications enable participants to exchange files during a session.
Integrated text-based messaging	Integrated text-based messaging enables participants to communicate in real time through private and public text-based chat.
Integrated video	Integrated video enables participants to share a video feed from a web cam.
Integrated Voice over Internet Protocol (VoIP) audio	Integrated VoIP audio enables two-way voice conversation among participants directly through the connected computer rather than a separate telephone connection. For some remote users, using VoIP audio directly through their computer may be an attractive alternative to using telephone for the audio connection, especially if the only telephone they have access to in their learning environment is a cell phone.

Session archiving	Session archiving provides an audio/video recording of various media shared through web conferencing. This can be useful for recording training sessions for review and to share with those who were unable to attend.
Polling and questioning	Polling and questioning features enable participants to post responses to impromptu questions.
Breakout rooms	Breakout rooms provide a session within the session that enables participates to temporarily split off into a separate sub-session where they can collaborate separately from other participates and return to the main session when they are done.

Other Conferencing and Collaboration Tools

In addition to web conferencing tools, you may choose to use additional tools to support conferencing and collaboration, especially in regard to activities before and after the training session itself.

Web-conferencing tools are typically session-based. That is, to be available for participants, a facilitator must start a session and students must log in to that session. When the session ends, access to the tools ends. This approach works acceptably in support of learning sessions that occur in an agreed-upon time, but may not work well for ad-hoc or asynchronous learning before or after a session. You can initiate an ad hoc web conferencing session or you can use other tools to support learning and collaboration outside of a web conferencing session.

Furthermore, you may find that the tools integrated within a web conferencing system may not completely meet your needs. Or you may already have other tools in place, such as a standalone text messaging system that your organization has standardized on. You may choose to supplement web conferencing tools with other standalone tools to assemble a system that will work best for you and your learners.

Social network sites	Social networking web sites provide features that supplement (and to some extent overlap) those found in web conferencing tools. Example sites include LinkedIn, Facebook, and Google+. Whereas web conferencing tools tend to be session-based (lending themselves to synchronous learning), features of most social networking sites tend to be asynchronous. Social networking sites may provide a good tool for asynchronous communication among class participants before and after a course.
Email	Email provides an always-on way to communicate outside of a class session. It can provide a useful way to provide support to learners beyond a class session. If you use email this way you may find it beneficial to set up a separate account exclusively for this purpose, to keep it separate from your normal email.

File sharing	Numerous cloud-based file-sharing services are available. These may be easier for many users to use than FTP or other traditional file-sharing tools.
Standalone communication and collaboration tools	Some of the features in web conferencing tools are available in stand-alone products, such as remote desktop sharing tools, text messaging, VoIP audio and video conferencing, discussion boards, and so forth. In many cases, you do not have to set up a special session to use them, so such programs may be suitable for one on one support after class—especially if all of the course participants already have such tools in place.

Other Classroom Technology Needs

Other technologies that you may need to configure your connected classroom include the following.

Individual web cams	Each participant is represented in the web conferencing software through a web cam directed at their face so other participants can see and interact with them. If possible, even students in the classroom should have a face cam so they can interact with remote students on an equal basis.
Classroom video	The classroom may also have one or more classroom cameras to provide different views of the classroom environment.
Alternate audio approaches	Audio conferencing by telephone is a tried-and-true technology, and many participants have extensive experience using such systems. This can provide an effective alternative to using special microphones or web cam audio in the classroom. Furthermore, some learners may not have microphones in the environment where they will be taking the course, but may have telephone access.
In-class projection systems	An in-class projection system can provide you with a way to share your presentation screen with local learners. The monitor can be shared with remote learners through web conferencing tools.
Interactive whiteboard	This is a projection monitor or large display monitor that provides a touch or pen interface that enables you to interact with the large display as though you were using a mouse. Typically, such devices include other capabilities, such as markup, the ability to draw on top of the currently displayed screen.

Remote labs   Virtual labs can support hands-on learning, even in situations where
                               providing direct access to software and hardware may be a challenge.

The LogicalCHOICE Experience

Your training materials should recognize and support the choices you have, and should accommodate and support your needs. In recognition of this, Logical Operations has developed the Logical-
CHOICE product line. For each course in the series, LogicalCHOICE includes print and e-book
editions of the facilitator's manual, printed and e-book editions of the student manuals, and online
resources presented through the LogicalCHOICE Platform.

The LogicalCHOICE Platform

LogicalCHOICE includes a collection of online resources that provide a key component of the
LogicalCHOICE learning experience and serve as the launch pad for various resources used in the
course. Students and facilitators log in to access course resources on the LogicalCHOICE Course
screen, the home page for a particular course. The LogicalCHOICE Course Screen is configurable.
The personal responsible for configuring courses in your organization can use the administrator
account to configure the platform according to your organization's needs.

The LogicalCHOICE Course screen provides access to the following class resources:

- *Ebook*, an interactive electronic version of the printed book for your course, which can be
  loaded and viewed from a variety of platforms including iPad®/iOS, Android®, Windows®
  tablets, and other devices.

- *LearnTOs*, animated components that enhance and extend the classroom learning experience.

- A link to the web conferencing session for the course.

- Links to social collaboration sites associated with the course.

- Student Whiteboard for sketches and notes.

- Link to virtual labs, which provide access to the technical environment for your course.

- Checklists with useful post-class reference information, such as procedure references.

- Notices from the LogicalCHOICE administrator.

- Course files.

Other resources provided through the LogicalCHOICE Platform include:

- The course assessment.

- Newsletters and other communications from the learning provider to learners.

- Mentoring services.

- A link to the training provider web site.

- The LogicalCHOICE store.

The following resources are considered core to the course, and will always be available to students, regardless of customization: ebook, LearnTOs, course files, course assessment, and checklists.

The LogicalCHOICE Student Edition Manual

The student manual documents the training experience for the learner, providing a complete reference of the material covered in the course. The student manual is available to the learner in both ebook and print form so the learner can use whatever format she or he finds most convenient. The student manual:

- Is divided into lessons and topics that cover the subject matter, with lessons typically arranged in order of increasing proficiency.

- Covers results-oriented topics that include relevant and supporting information you need to master the content.

- Provides extensive activities and discussions designed to enable you to practice the guidelines and procedures as well as to solidify your understanding of the informational material presented in the course.

- Provides concise procedure references and guidelines.

- Includes reflective activities and practice labs to reinforce learning and promote higher order thinking.

- Includes data files and supporting files for this course, available by download from the LogicalCHOICE Course Screen, which is accessible via an access key provided in an email for each unit ordered.

- Includes a glossary of the definitions of the terms and concepts used throughout the course.

- Includes a table of contents and index to assist in locating information within the instructional components of the book.

The LogicalCHOICE Instructor's Edition

The LogicalCHOICE Instructor's Edition is essentially the Student Edition extended with features that support the class facilitator and others involved in setting up and delivering the course. The additional features of a LogicalCHOICE Facilitator's Edition include:

Course setup   Course setup notes describe hardware and software requirements for the facilitator and student computers, and include step by step instructions to prepare computers for the class.

Course-specific delivery tips   Supplemental content and delivery tips provide the facilitator with additional insights to deliver the course successfully.

Presentation planners   Presentation planners help the facilitator plan the class schedule, and include examples of a continuous schedule (e.g. over one day) and an extended schedule (e.g. four, 90-minute sessions).

Facilitator notes   In the page margins, the facilitator edition includes notes and tips to the facilitator. The following types of notes are provided.

 A **display slide** note provides a prompt to the instructor to display a specific slide from the provided PowerPoint files.

 Content delivery tips provide guidance for specific delivery techniques you may want to utilize at particular points in the course, such as lectures, whiteboard sketching, or performing your own demonstrations for the class.

 Managing learning interactions provides notes on suggested places to interact with the class as a whole. You might poll the class with close-ended questions, check comprehension with open-ended questions, conduct planned discussion activities, or take notes and questions from the group to "park" and address at a later point in the class.

 Monitoring learner progress notes suggest when you might want to monitor individual students as they perform activities, or have private "sidebar" conversations with specific individual participants.

 Engaging learners notes suggest opportunities to involve the students in active ways with the course presentation, such as enabling them to demonstrate their work to the class as a whole, or checking in on the logistics of the presentation.

Incorporating other assets notes suggest when and how to include other types of media, such as visiting LogicalCHOICE social media sites, accessing specific web resources, or utilizing media assets provided with the course, such as Logical Operations' LearnTOs.

 Additional notes show where, on occasion, there may be instructor notes or tips that appear in a separate section at the back of the courseware and not in the margins.

Delivering a LogicalCHOICE Course

Although LogicalCHOICE provides a thorough, tested solution for delivering instructor-led training, as with any course, the key to delivering the best possible training is to be prepared. Not only should you understand the subject matter, but you should be thoroughly familiar with the course content and materials. You should take steps to ensure that everything is ready for the day of class. Following are guidelines to help you prepare.

Before You Deliver the Class the First Time

Before you teach the class for the first time, perform the following steps to prepare.

Learn to Use Your Web Conferencing Tool

Be sure to also plan for any additional time it will take you to learn new tools. For example, if you're using a web conferencing system to present to remote learners, make sure that you know how to:

- Schedule a web conferencing session and invite other participants.

- Display a slide presentation.

- Display the whiteboard.

- Share an application or the desktop.

- Pass control of the application to another participant in the session.

- Point at and mark up the display so that remote learners can see what you're pointing at or talking about. (You should be able to do this with slides, whiteboard, or a shared application screen.)

- Exchange files with remote learners.

Get to the Know the Course and Make It Your Own

Before you teach a class for the first time, perform the following steps:

1. Become thoroughly familiar with the course materials.

    - At your desk (or wherever you work best), work through the course like a student, keying through each activity in sequence so you know what students will do in class as you lead them.

    - Note any lead-ins, transitions, and storylines you will use in delivery, and add or enhance with your own ideas.

    - Make notes in your Instructor's Edition to add your own ideas.

    - If you will have remote learners, consider how you will keep them engaged and note any accommodations you may need to make to create the best possible learning experience.

    - Read and consider the notes provided in the Instructor's Edition to call out areas where you may want to focus on aspects of content delivery, managing learner interactions, engaging learners, monitoring learner progress, and incorporating other assets. Add your own notes in the margins as needed.

2. Prepare your slides. As you work through the course materials, each time you encounter an instructor note calling for a slide, look at the corresponding slide in the course materials so you know how to present it. Add your own slides where you think they are appropriate. Add margin notes to indicate where your new slides appear, and mark existing slide notes to indicate those you don't wish to use.

3. Prepare question postings. If you're using a web conferencing system to deliver the course, you may wish to create import files containing any polling and quiz questions you plan to use during the session.

4. Prepare a file set. Although you may the classroom and web conferencing environment set up before class, it's always good to plan for contingencies. Keep an extra set of files handy for anything you may need to retrieve during class. Put your files in a network location, cloud storage, thumb drive, or some other location where you will able to access them in class. Files you may wish to have on hand include PowerPoint files for the course, student data, any web shortcuts you plan to use, additional media and example documents you may wish to share, polling questions, and anything else you might want to refer to.

Before You Deliver the Class Each Time

Each time you deliver the class, perform the following steps before the class begins. Be sure to do this well ahead of the class start time so you can deal with any technical problems that might occur.

1. Perform the course setup. Course setup requirements and instructions are provided in the Instructor's Edition of the course. If you delegate this task to someone else, you may wish to verify the class setup has been done correctly. If you have remote learners, send them (or whoever will set up their system) with the course setup instructions well enough in advance of class that they have time to do so.

2. Set up the conferencing session. If you will use web conferencing software, send a session invitation to all participants. If you know you will have students who have not used a web conferencing system before, plan this into the class schedule.

3. Book the classroom. If you're using shared space for your local classroom, verify that the room is available and assigned to your class.

The Day of the Class

Perform the following steps on the day of the class.

1. As you begin class, orient learners to the ground rules of working with web conferencing tools, how to participate, and so forth. For example:

    - If you're using audio/video conferencing, the slight communication delay in the call may cause learners to talk over each other. It can also be confusing for participants to know who's talking. Some conferencing tools highlight on screen the name of the participant who is currently talking. For other systems, it may be good to have learners lead in with "Hi, this is [*student name*]" before they begin speaking.

    - Tell students how to set up their web conferencing windows for the best experience. If you're teaching a hands-on computer training course, it may be beneficial to have them show the web conferencing tools in a window (rather than in full screen mode) so they can arrange the tools in a way that enables them to easily switch between their application window (for hands-on activities) and the conferencing windows (for discussion, interaction, and to view shared slides and demos).

2. If learners are not familiar with the web conferencing tool, provide them with an orientation to the tool. You can do this within the ongoing context of class, introducing and explaining each feature as you use it for the first time.

3. Once you have shared your screen, orient students to the LogicalCHOICE Course screen, pointing out any components you plan to use in your class:

    - eBook – The interactive electronic version of the course manual

    - LearnTOs – Supplemental course content in the form of animated multimedia

    - The virtual classroom for the course

    - Social media resources related to the course

    - Personal whiteboard for sketches and notes

    - Virtual labs, for remote access to the technical environment for your course

    - Checklists with useful post-class reference information

    - The course assessment

    - Newsletters and other communications from your training organization

- Mentoring services

- A link to the website of your training provider

- The LogicalCHOICE store

4. Provide learners with the URL for the LogicalCHOICE Course creen and with their login information.

5. Have learners open their ebook or print manual, and explain how the manual is laid out:

- The manual is divided into lessons and topics that cover the subject matter, with lessons typically arranged in order of increasing proficiency.

- The results-oriented topics include relevant and supporting information you need to master the content. Each topic has various types of activities designed to enable you to practice the guidelines and procedures as well as to solidify your understanding of the informational material presented in the course. Procedures and guidelines are presented in a concise fashion along with activities and discussions. Information is provided for reference and reflection in such a way as to facilitate understanding and practice.

- Datafiles for various activities as well as other supporting files for the course are available by download from the LogicalCHOICE Course screen.

- At the back of the book, you will find a glossary of the definitions of the terms and concepts used throughout the course. You will also find an index to assist in locating information within the instructional components of the book.

6. As you present the course, you have many tasks to attend to. In addition to the activities any instructor must perform, you will also need to keep the classroom technology configured and ensure that all of your learners, local and remote, are engaged and operating effectively. The following Presentation Best Practices provide some guidance in this challenging process.

Presentation Best Practices

Delivering courses in the connected classroom may provide benefits beyond just providing you and your students with choice of scheduling and location. Enhancements to support better communication among participants and promote active learning, while aimed at making distance learning a better experience, will likely improve the experience for all learners, both remote and local.

Teaching in the connected classroom can take some adjustment at first. Learners bring different aptitudes, attitudes, experience, and skills. Meeting the needs of all students all the time has always been a challenge. Add to that the challenge of facilitating learning from a distance, and it becomes apparent that the attributes of a successful trainer—subject matter knowledge, planning, communication skills, learner focus, classroom time management, and so forth—are more important than ever.

Promote Active Learning

Slides, screen images, and other presentation graphics are useful for presenting material that is abstract or that can't be easily shown in the classroom context. As needed, you can add your own slides to those included in LogicalCHOICE. However, avoid adding so many slides that your course becomes heavy on lecture and light on activity. If you want to cover supplemental content, look first for ways that you can deliver it through guided hands-on activities or demonstrations. When learners *interact* with new ideas, rather than just trying to absorb and memorize them, they maintain interest and attention. When possible, enable learners to experience activities for themselves, rather than simply talking about them or demonstrating them.

Software Demonstrations

Screen sharing software enables you to share your screen with students who are remote. There can also be benefits for students who are local. Because the image is shown directly on their own screen, visibility isn't subject to limitations in the room based on lighting, distance from the projected display, and so forth. Furthermore some screen-sharing systems provide built-in session recording so you can save a video which learners can refer to for review. If your facilitator environment provides screen markup capabilities, use this to advantage. For example, to help students attend to a particular icon or portion of the screen as you guide them through a hands-on activity, use your markup tools to highlight the portion of the screen they should attend to.

Parking Lot

As you progress through the course, learners may ask questions for which you do not have an immediate answer. Or they may ask a question for which you have an answer, but you want to wait until other topics have been covered before you address the question. In such cases, it isn't sufficient to simply put off the answer until later. To assure students that all of their questions will be addressed, you can create a parking lot, where you will note these questions to assure students they will all be addressed. Later on, when you reach the proper point to address the question (or after you have researched the answer during a break in instruction), you can circle back to the parking lot, answer the question, and check it off as having been answered. The tool you use to record parking lot questions could be as simple as notes you type into Windows Notepad or another simple text editor. You can display the parking lot questions on the presentation monitor if there is room there, or you can position it on your private monitor, and periodically move it back into view on the presentation monitor as you review existing questions and add new ones.

Use Questioning and Polling Tools

Web conferencing tools such as polling, questioning, and even the simple but effective **raise your hand** button provide you with a quick way to take a reading on how every learner is doing. Of course, as in the traditional classroom, you may ask learners how they are doing and you receive back an all-too-quick response, "we're doing fine." If you're not convinced that they really are doing fine, deliver a quick skill check: use your web conferencing tool to pose a quick question about content you just covered, or observe their performance closely in the next activity. The LogicalCHOICE Instructor's Edition provides notes with examples of where to insert questions and polls.

Level the Playing Field

Set up the classroom environment and when possible ensure that learner environments are configured so there is no disadvantage to being remote or local. As you deliver the course, try to use the same tools whenever possible for dialogue, questioning, polling, and so forth to enable all students to participate equally.

Keep aware of how you're communicating. If you're acting out visually, using your hands or facial expressions, drawing or highlighting, make sure you do these things directly on your web cam video or on the presentation monitor where they will be seen by all students. Also remember that the typically slow frame rate of web video will blur fast movements or subtle gestures, which will not translate well to online delivery.

Monitor and Adjust Frequently

 As a human being delivering training, you have an immediate advantage over e-learning and other forms of self-study. You have an innate ability to sense affect: how learners are doing, whether they are getting it, and whether they are struggling to keep up. Take advantage of your ability to sense how learners are doing, and adjust your delivery as needed. Use activities and lesson labs provided in the LogicalCHOICE course as a chance to monitor student performance.

Activities and lesson labs provide a good opportunity to check learner progress. If you suspect a learner is having trouble, you can use this time to have them share their screens privately with you so you can see how they're doing. A private chat message may also be sufficient as a way to check in with individual students.

Make Eye Contact

Assuming your learners have face-cams (individual web cams for each student), don't forget to look into their faces as you present. Although making eye contact may be a natural thing to do when all of your learners are local, it is easy to neglect to do this when you have remote learners. Make sure the video monitor with the face-cam videos is located where you can see it while you're presenting. You can tell a lot simply by looking at the expressions on the faces of your learners.

Use Dialogue

If you do all of the talking, you won't have a good sense of what students are thinking. In many situations, you can walk alongside students to take them where you want them to go through discussion, rather than simply carrying them there through lecture.

For example, rather than say "this Excel formula works perfectly except for this one place," you might say "Is this Excel formula meeting our needs perfectly at this point? Is there one place where we might need to do something different?"

Both approaches will get learners to the same point, but there are benefits to selectively using dialogue at times rather than always using lecture. Dialogue promotes active learning by increasing the effort of thought that learners must exert to get to the answer. Dialogue also gives you a sense of students' understanding. If nobody gets it, it will be immediately apparent through the ideas they communicate (or the silence).

Show and Tell

Because lesson labs are not as tightly scripted as guided activities, there will likely be more variation in the results produced by learners. If time permits, you might consider having students volunteer to share their desktops to show their results and explain what they did to produce them.

Build Flexibility Into the Class Schedule

Build flexibility into your class schedule so you can monitor students' progress through the course and adjust as needed. Just as a balloonist carries sandbags that can be released as needed when the balloon falls short on lift, consider including optional material in your class schedule that you can use or not use depending on the pace of the class. The lesson labs, LearnTOs, and ad hoc social/interaction tips provided in the LogicalCHOICE course materials are a good source of such material. You may also want to build-in your own additional optional material, such as outside resources, field trips to relevant websites, or demos that you can incorporate into the class if there is adequate time. If you're training a homogeneous group, such as a group who all work in the same department, organization, or industry, you may use this as an opportunity to add content that has been customized for this specific group.

Schedule adequate hours to account for the time these extras will require in the best case scenario, where students move through the course quickly. In anything less than the best case scenario, you can omit the extra material to gain back some time in the schedule. Be upfront with students and tell them at the beginning of the class that you will cover all of the material in the course, but depending on the timing of the class, you may not have time during the class for students to complete every lesson lab or the other extras. The labs are designed to be completed independently and include all of the files needed. If they want, students can perform the lesson labs any time after the class if they wish to gain additional practice.

Considering directing learners to related blog sites, wikis, discussion sites, and other useful web resources. You can provide links to other resources through the LogicalCHOICE Course screen. The LogicalCHOICE Course screen also provides additional resources that you can utilize to support additional learning or reference after the class, such as LearnTO videos, procedure references, and checklists.

After Class

 After you have finished the class, follow up by participating in social media sites that you have set up for the course. You have the choice to use the social media sites you and your learners prefer. Ideas for ways that you can engage learners after class include:

- Post or tweet additional tips and hints for learning beyond the course.

- Provide a forum in which learners can post follow-up questions about material covered in the course, where you and others can provide them with answers.

- Provide opportunities for learners to post examples of ways in which they are applying what was covered in the course.

- Provide information and notifications on other courses learners may be interested in.

- Promote communities of practice by providing a forum in which learners can support and share information with each other.

Conclusion: Making the Transition to Virtual

The benefits offered by the connected classroom are significant. More organizations are taking advantage of the opportunities offered by new technologies and are delivering high quality instructor led training while offering more flexibility. Take advantage of information and activities provided in your CHOICE course materials. As you teach in the connected classroom, you will develop additional techniques beyond those presented here to take advantage of the technology and to promote active learning for all of your students. Continually learn from your experience and share your ideas.

Logical Operations provides an online community and resource center where instructors from all over the world share their ideas, interact, and engage each other. Visit www.linkedin.com to join our group, the Logical Operations Instructor Community. Also, receive free access to a CHOICE instructor course made specifically for you – visit www.lo-choice.com and enter access key **LCSYB24YEF** .

Again, congratulations on your choice – the right choice – the Logical CHOICE!

Microsoft® Office PowerPoint® 2010: Part 2

Microsoft® Office PowerPoint® 2010: Part 2

Part Number: 091032
Course Edition: 2.2

Acknowledgements

PROJECT TEAM

Author	Media Designer	Content Editor
Tim Barnosky	Alex Tong	Catherine M. Albano

Notices

DISCLAIMER

TRADEMARK NOTICES

Microsoft® Office PowerPoint® 2010: Part 2

Modifying the PowerPoint Environment..1

    Customize the User Interface.. 2

    Set PowerPoint 2010 Options... 10

Customizing Design Templates.. 15

    Modify Slide Masters and Slide Layouts.....................................16

    Add Headers and Footers... 22

    Modify the Notes Master and the Handout Master.........................26

Adding SmartArt to a Presentation...31

    Create SmartArt...32

    Modify SmartArt.. 36

Working with Media and Animations...41

    Add Audio to a Presentation...42

    Add Video to a Presentation... 47

    Customize Animations and Transitions.. 52

Collaborating on a Presentation...59

    Review a Presentation..60

    Publish Slides to a Slide Library.. 68

    Share a Presentation on the Web.. 71

Customizing a Slide Show... 77

    Annotate a Presentation... 78

    Set Up a Slide Show... 81

    Create a Custom Slide Show... 85

    Add Hyperlinks and Action Buttons... 88

    Record a Presentation.. 92

Securing and Distributing a Presentation.. 97

    Secure a Presentation.. 98

    Broadcast a Slide Show.. 103

    Create a Video or a CD... 107

Appendix A: Microsoft Office PowerPoint 2010 Exam 77-883............. 115

Appendix B: Microsoft PowerPoint 2010 Common Keyboard Shortcuts 123

Lesson Labs.. 125

Glossary... 133

Index... 137

Using the Microsoft® Office PowerPoint® 2010: Part 2 Instructor's Edition

Welcome to the Instructor

Welcome and congratulations on your choice to use the finest materials available on the market today for expert-facilitated learning in any presentation modality. You can utilize the *Microsoft® Office PowerPoint® 2010: Part 2* curriculum to present world-class instructional experiences whether:

- Your students are with you in the classroom, or participating virtually.
- You are presenting in a continuous event, or in an extended teaching plan, such as an academic semester.
- Your presentation takes place synchronously with the students, or asynchronously.
- Your students have physical courseware, or are using digital materials.
- You have any combination of these instructional dimensions.

To make the best use of the *Microsoft® Office PowerPoint® 2010: Part 2* materials in any or all of these dimensions, be sure to review the contents of the LogicalCHOICE Facilitator's Guide for an orientation to all of the components of the LogicalCHOICE experience.

Preparing to Present the LogicalCHOICE Experience

Effectively presenting the information and skills in this course requires adequate preparation, no matter your presentation modality. As such, as an instructor, you should familiarize yourself with the content of the entire course, including its organization and instructional approaches. You should review each of the student activities and exercises so you can facilitate them during the learning event. Make sure you review all of the instructor tips for presenting in the different dimensions that are available in the margins of your Instructor's Edition.

In addition to the curriculum itself, Microsoft® PowerPoint® slides, data files, and other course-specific support material may be available by downloading the files from the LogicalCHOICE Course screen. Be sure to obtain the course files prior to your learning event and make sure you distribute them to your students.

Course Facilitator Icons

Throughout the Instructor's Edition, you may see various instructor-focused icons that provide suggestions, answers to problems, and supplemental information for you, the instructor.

Icon	Description
	A **display slide** note provides a prompt to the instructor to display a specific slide from the provided PowerPoint files.
	Content delivery tips provide guidance for specific delivery techniques you may want to utilize at particular points in the course, such as lectures, whiteboard sketching, or performing your own demonstrations for the class.
	Managing learning interactions provides notes on suggested places to interact with the class as a whole. You might poll the class with closed-ended questions, check comprehension with open-ended questions, conduct planned discussion activities, or take notes and questions from the group to "park" and address at a later point in the class.
	Monitoring learner progress notes suggest when you might want to monitor individual students as they perform activities, or have private "sidebar" conversations with specific individual participants.
	Engaging learners notes suggest opportunities to involve the students in active ways with the course presentation, such as enabling them to demonstrate their work to the class as a whole, or checking in on the logistics of the presentation.
	Incorporating other assets notes suggest when and how to include other types of media, such as visiting LogicalCHOICE social media sites, accessing specific web resources, or utilizing media assets provided with the course, such as Logical Operations' LearnTOs.
	Additional notes show where, on occasion, there may be instructor notes or tips that appear in a separate section at the back of the courseware and not in the margins.

Course-Specific Technical Requirements

Hardware

For this course, you will need one computer for each student and one for the instructor. Each computer will need the following minimum hardware configurations:

- 1 GHz or faster 32-bit (x86) or 64-bit (x64) processor
- 1 gigabyte (GB) RAM (32-bit) or 2 GB RAM (64-bit)
- 16 GB available hard disk space (32-bit) or 20 GB (64-bit)
- DirectX 9.0c graphics card with 64 MB or higher of video memory recommended
- Audio output device and speakers or headphones
- CD-ROM drive
- Keyboard and mouse (or other pointing device)
- 1024 × 768 resolution monitor recommended
- Network cards and cabling for local network access
- Internet access (contact your local network administrator)
- Printer (optional) or an installed printer driver
- Projection system to display the instructor's computer screen

Software

- Microsoft® Office Professional Edition 2010

- Microsoft® Office Suite Service Pack 1
- Microsoft® Windows® 7 Professional with Service Pack 1

Setting Up the Course

For each student and the instructor:

- Provide a system with Internet access and the given hardware requirements.
- Install Microsoft® Windows® 7 Professional. Ensure the operating system has been updated with Service Pack 1.
- Install Microsoft® Office Professional Edition 2010.
- Install Microsoft® Office Suite Service Pack 1.
- Ensure there is an available active Windows Live ID and a Windows SkyDrive account (**https://skydrive.live.com/**).
- Launch Windows.

Students may use existing Microsoft accounts for the activities in this course. You may wish to contact the students before class to determine whether or not they need an account. You can choose to set up accounts for students who require them, or you may ask the students to set them up ahead of time. Microsoft accounts are free of charge. If students wish to delete accounts created for the purposes of this course, they may do so at **https://login.live.com/**. To deactivate the accounts, students will need to log in using their credentials, select **Close account** from the bottom of the **Account summary** page, and then follow the prompts.

In order to participate in the optional activity in Lesson 5 Topic B, you and the students will require access to an existing Microsoft SharePoint site with a Slide Library. Check with your network/ systems administrator for availability and access privileges. This activity also requires Microsoft Office PowerPoint Professional Plus 2010. To view the PowerPoint Professional Plus 2010 system requirements, visit **http://technet.microsoft.com/en-us/library/ee624351.aspx**.

As some of the data files for this course have similar names, it may be useful to ensure that file extensions are always displayed in Windows 7. To set this option:

1. Select **Start→Control Panel**.
2. Select **Appearance and Personalization**, and then select **Folder Options**.
3. In the **Folder Options** dialog box, select the **View** tab.
4. Uncheck the **Hide extensions for known file types** check box.
5. Select **OK**.

After each class session, in order to ensure all activities key properly, reset the following to their default states/settings:

1. The ribbon and the **Quick Access Toolbar**.

   - Launch PowerPoint 2010.
   - Select **File→Options→Customize Ribbon**.
   - In the **PowerPoint Options** dialog box, in the **Customizations** section, select **Reset**, and then select **Reset all customizations**.
   - In the Microsoft Office dialog box, select **Yes**.

2. The maximum number of undos.

   - In the **PowerPoint Options** dialog box, select the **Advanced** tab.
   - In the **Editing options** section, in the **Maximum number of undos** field, use the spin buttons to set the value to 20.

3. The number of displayed recent documents.

   - In the **PowerPoint Options** dialog box, ensure the **Advanced** tab is selected.
   - In the **Display** section, in the **Show this number of Recent Documents** field, use the spin buttons to set the value to 20.
   - Select **OK**.

• Close PowerPoint 2010.

Install the Course Data Files

From the location you downloaded the course data files to, open the 091032 folder. Then open the Data folder. Run the 091032dd.exe file in that folder, which will install a folder named 091032Data at the root of your C: drive. This folder contains all the data files you will need to run this course. There is a separate folder with the starter files for each lesson or lab, and there may be a Solutions folder containing completed files that students can use to check their results.

Presentation Planners

The lesson durations given in the course content are estimates based on a typical class experience. The following planners show examples of how the content could be presented in either a continuous one-day flow or separately across a multi-session seminar series. Your presentation flow may vary based on a number of factors, including the size of the class, whether students are in specialized job roles, whether you plan to incorporate LearnTOs or other assets from the LogicalCHOICE Course screen into the course, and so on. Use the samples and blank planners to determine how you will conduct the class to meet the needs of your own situation.

Continuous Presentation: Model Class Flow

This planner provides a sample presentation flow based on one 6.5-hour day of training, with breaks and lunch factored in.

Section	Duration	Day Planner
Welcome and Introductions	0:10	8:30 – 8:40
Lesson 1: Modifying the PowerPoint Environment	0:40	8:40 – 9:20
Lesson 2: Customizing Design Templates	0:45	9:20 – 10:05
Lesson 3: Adding SmartArt to a Presentation	0:40	10:05 – 10:45
BREAK	0:15	10:45 – 11:00
Lesson 4: Working with Media and Animations	1:15	11:00 – 12:15
LUNCH	0:30	12:15 – 12:45
Lesson 5: Collaborating on a Presentation	1:10	12:45 – 1:55
Lesson 6: Customizing a Slide Show	1:00	1:55 – 2:55
BREAK	0:15	2:55 – 3:10
Lesson 7: Securing and Distributing a Presentation	0:50	3:10 – 4:00

Continuous Presentation: Your Class Flow

Use this planner to plan the flow of your own training day, based on the needs of your students, the schedule for your own day, and/or any other modifications you choose.

Section	Duration	Day Planner
Welcome and Introductions		
Lesson 1: Modifying the PowerPoint Environment		
Lesson 2: Customizing Design Templates		
Lesson 3: Adding SmartArt to a Presentation		
Lesson 4: Working with Media and Animations		
Lesson 5: Collaborating on a Presentation		
Lesson 6: Customizing a Slide Show		
Lesson 7: Securing and Distributing a Presentation		

Non-continuous Presentation: Model Class Flow

This planner provides a sample presentation flow based on separate sessions presented over multiple days or weeks.

Session Number	Material Covered	Session Duration
One	Welcome and Introductions Lesson 1: Modifying the PowerPoint Environment Lesson 2: Customizing Design Templates	1:35
Two	Lesson 3: Adding SmartArt to a Presentation Lesson 4: Working with Media and Animations	1:55
Three	Lesson 5: Collaborating on a Presentation	1:10
Four	Lesson 6: Customizing a Slide Show Lesson 7: Securing and Distributing a Presentation	1:50

Non-continuous Presentation: Your Class Flow

Use this planner to plan how you will present the course content, based on the needs of your students, your conventions for the number and length of sessions, and any other modifications you choose.

Session Number	Material Covered	Session Duration

About This Course

Meetings, instruction, training, pitches; these are all a part of our daily lives. We are often called upon to deliver presentations with little notice, at multiple venues, and with varying requirements, and that includes sensitive information that needs to be guarded. Given all the variables, it may seem an overwhelming task to deliver your content, on time, to all audiences, and to only those who need to see it. Oh, and by the way, you need to make it interesting, informative, and memorable. So, how do you do it? Without the help of a robust set of tools, it would be nearly impossible. But, PowerPoint 2010 provides you with a variety of such tools, that can help you deliver content in nearly any situation, while saving time and effort.

By taking advantage of these tools, you will be creating presentations that not only stand out from the crowd, but also don't consume all of your available time.

Course Description

Target Student

This course is intended for students who have a foundational working knowledge of PowerPoint 2010, who wish to take advantage of the application's higher-level usability, security, collaboration, and distribution functionality.

Course Prerequisites

To ensure success, students should have experience using PowerPoint 2010, running within the Windows 7 operating system, to create, edit, and deliver multimedia presentations. To attain this level of knowledge and skills, you can take the following Logical Operations courses:

- *Microsoft® Windows® 7: Level 1* or *Windows® 7: Transition from Windows® XP*
- *Microsoft® Office PowerPoint® 2010: Part 1*

Course Objectives

Upon completing this course, you will be able to customize the PowerPoint 2010 application, and effectively create, collaborate on, secure, and distribute complex multimedia presentations for a variety of situations.

You will:

- Modify the PowerPoint environment.
- Customize design templates.
- Add SmartArt to a presentation.
- Work with media and animations.
- Collaborate on a presentation.

- Customize a slide show.
- Secure and distribute a presentation.

The LogicalCHOICE Home Screen

http://www.lo-choice.com

The LogicalCHOICE Home screen is your entry point to the LogicalCHOICE learning experience, of which this course manual is only one part. Visit the LogicalCHOICE Course screen both during and after class to make use of the world of support and instructional resources that make up the LogicalCHOICE experience.

Log-on and access information for your LogicalCHOICE environment will be provided with your class experience. On the LogicalCHOICE Home screen, you can access the LogicalCHOICE Course screens for your specific courses.

Each LogicalCHOICE Course screen will give you access to the following resources:

- eBook: an interactive electronic version of the printed book for your course.
- LearnTOs: brief animated components that enhance and extend the classroom learning experience.

Depending on the nature of your course and the choices of your learning provider, the LogicalCHOICE Course screen may also include access to elements such as:

- The interactive eBook.
- Social media resources that enable you to collaborate with others in the learning community using professional communications sites such as LinkedIn or microblogging tools such as Twitter.
- Checklists with useful post-class reference information.
- Any course files you will download.
- The course assessment.
- Notices from the LogicalCHOICE administrator.
- Virtual labs, for remote access to the technical environment for your course.
- Your personal whiteboard for sketches and notes.
- Newsletters and other communications from your learning provider.
- Mentoring services.
- A link to the website of your training provider.
- The LogicalCHOICE store.

Visit your LogicalCHOICE Home screen often to connect, communicate, and extend your learning experience!

How to Use This Book

As You Learn

This book is divided into lessons and topics, covering a subject or a set of related subjects. In most cases, lessons are arranged in order of increasing proficiency.

The results-oriented topics include relevant and supporting information you need to master the content. Each topic has various types of activities designed to enable you to practice the guidelines and procedures as well as to solidify your understanding of the informational material presented in the course. Procedures and guidelines are presented in a concise fashion along with activities and discussions. Information is provided for reference and reflection in such a way as to facilitate understanding and practice.

Data files for various activities as well as other supporting files for the course are available by download from the LogicalCHOICE Course screen. In addition to sample data for the course exercises, the course files may contain media components to enhance your learning and additional reference materials for use both during and after the course.

At the back of the book, you will find a glossary of the definitions of the terms and concepts used throughout the course. You will also find an index to assist in locating information within the instructional components of the book.

As You Review

Any method of instruction is only as effective as the time and effort you, the student, are willing to invest in it. In addition, some of the information that you learn in class may not be important to you immediately, but it may become important later. For this reason, we encourage you to spend some time reviewing the content of the course after your time in the classroom.

As a Reference

The organization and layout of this book make it an easy-to-use resource for future reference. Taking advantage of the glossary, index, and table of contents, you can use this book as a first source of definitions, background information, and summaries.

Course Icons

Watch throughout the material for these visual cues:

Icon	Description
	A **Note** provides additional information, guidance, or hints about a topic or task.
	A **Caution** helps make you aware of places where you need to be particularly careful with your actions, settings, or decisions so that you can be sure to get the desired results of an activity or task.
	LearnTO notes show you where an associated LearnTO is particularly relevant to the content. Access LearnTOs from your LogicalCHOICE Course screen.
	Checklists provide job aids you can use after class as a reference to performing skills back on the job. Access checklists from your LogicalCHOICE Course screen.
	Social notes remind you to check your LogicalCHOICE Course screen for opportunities to interact with the LogicalCHOICE community using social media.
	Notes Pages are intentionally left blank for you to write on.

1 | Modifying the PowerPoint Environment

Lesson Time: 40 minutes

Lesson Objectives

In this lesson, you will modify the PowerPoint environment. You will:

- Customize the user interface
- Set PowerPoint 2010 options

Lesson Introduction

For many PowerPoint 2010 users, the default settings and user interface provide an efficient, highly functional environment in which to create multimedia presentations. You may find, though, that you need some of the less commonly used commands for your particular purposes. Or, you may find that you frequently use commands that are in groups on separate tabs on the ribbon. There are also many cases in which saving files in particular formats proves more useful for you. Although the PowerPoint 2010 environment has been designed with ease-of-use and efficiency in mind, you will find that some configurations simply work better for certain purposes.

PowerPoint 2010 provides you with an array of options for modifying the environment you use to develop your presentations. From customizing the ribbon and other user interface elements, to setting options for file management and printing, you have a lot of control over how PowerPoint works for you. Getting familiar with what options are available, and how they can help you work faster with less effort, is perhaps the first step in becoming an advanced PowerPoint user.

TOPIC A

Customize the User Interface

As you work with PowerPoint 2010, you will find you use certain commands far more than others. This is often a function of your job role, the industry in which you work, or the type of presentation you have been asked to deliver. Because you have developed a level of comfort working within PowerPoint 2010, it may be to your advantage to customize the user interface to better suit your needs. You may also find it advantageous to have multiple presentations open at the same time. This will make comparing presentations, and copying and pasting slides or other content, far easier.

PowerPoint 2010 offers you a host of options for customizing the user interface, including the ribbon. Putting in a bit of effort to configure the PowerPoint environment according to your work flow can improve your efficiency and provide you with a more positive user experience.

The PowerPoint Options Dialog Box

The PowerPoint Options Dialog Box

The **PowerPoint Options** dialog box provides you with the various options for customizing the PowerPoint user interface and for setting application options. The **PowerPoint Options** dialog box is divided into nine tabs, which display the options for customizing your PowerPoint user experience. You can access the **PowerPoint Options** dialog box by selecting **File→Options**.

 Note: Logical Operations uses a streamlined notation for ribbon commands. They'll appear, for example, as "**Ribbon Tab→[Group]→Button or Control**," as in "select **Home→Clipboard→Paste**." If the group name isn't needed for navigation or there isn't a group, it's omitted, as in "select **File→Open**."

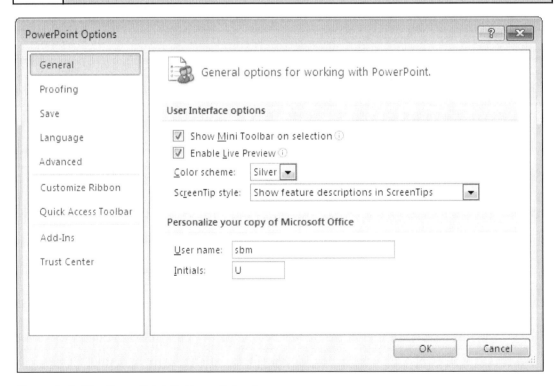

Figure 1-1: The PowerPoint Options dialog box.

Tab	Provides Options For
General	Displaying the **Mini** toolbar, enabling Live Preview, enabling ClearType, customizing the user interface color scheme, customizing screen tips, and setting the user name and initials.
Proofing	Customizing **AutoCorrect** and **Spell Checker** functionality. You can specify which spelling and grammatical errors PowerPoint should recognize, and how it should address them.
Save	Determining file formats and customizing auto-save options. You can also configure options for files stored on servers, and for sharing and merging files.
Language	Selecting edit, display, Help, and screen tip languages.
Advanced	Customizing editing features; cut, copy, and paste functionality; image settings; display settings; slide show functionality; and print settings.
Customize Ribbon	Arranging, adding, deleting, and customizing tabs, groups, and commands on the ribbon.
Quick Access Toolbar	Adding, deleting, and arranging commands on the **Quick Access Toolbar**.
Add-Ins	Viewing and managing installed applications that increase PowerPoint functionality.
Trust Center	Modifying the PowerPoint privacy and security settings.

The Customize Ribbon Tab

One of the quickest ways to improve your work flow is to customize the ribbon. The **Customize Ribbon** tab in the **PowerPoint Options** dialog box provides you with the commands to create the ideal ribbon environment to suit your needs. PowerPoint 2010 allows you to change the order of tabs and groups on the ribbon. You can also create custom tabs and groups, and reorder the commands on any of your custom groups. If you need to work from another computer, PowerPoint 2010 allows you to save ribbon customizations and import them on other machines.

The Customize Ribbon Tab

 Note: You can only add, remove, and reorder commands in custom groups. You can reorder all tabs and groups.

This is a good opportunity to poll the students about what they like or dislike about the ribbon. What would they change? Use the chat or whiteboard features of your web conferencing system if polling isn't available.

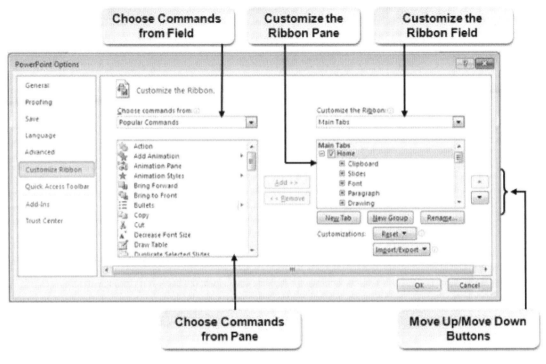

Figure 1-2: The Customize Ribbon tab.

Customize Ribbon Tab Element	Description
Choose Commands from Field	Populates the **Choose commands from pane** with commands from various command categories, such as popular commands, all commands, or commands from a particular tab.
Choose Commands from Pane	Displays commands you can add to custom groups and tabs on the ribbon.
Customize the Ribbon Field	Selects which tabs are available for customization. You can select from among the main commands, all commands, and tool (contextual) tabs.
Customize the Ribbon Pane	Displays tabs, groups, and commands as they appear on the ribbon.
Add	Moves the selected command in the **Choose commands from** pane to the selected group in the **Customize the Ribbon** pane.
Remove	Removes the selected command from its group in the **Customize the Ribbon** pane.
Move Up	Moves a tab, a group, or a command up in the **Customize the Ribbon** pane.
Move Down	Moves a tab, a group, or a command down in the **Customize the Ribbon** pane.
New Tab	Creates a new tab.
New Group	Creates a new group.
Rename	Allows you to rename a custom tab or group, or to rename a command within a custom group.

Customize Ribbon Tab Element	Description
Reset	Restores all or selected customizations to default settings.
Import/Export	Allows you to export customizations as a file or import saved customizations to another computer.

The Customize the Ribbon Pane Hierarchy

The **Customize the Ribbon** pane is arranged in a tree hierarchy. The top level of the tree represents the ribbon tabs. The groups are contained within the tabs, one level down in the hierarchy. The commands are contained within the groups. Commands with a drop-down menu contain another sub-level, which displays the commands that appear within the drop-down menu.

The Customize the Ribbon Pane Hierarchy

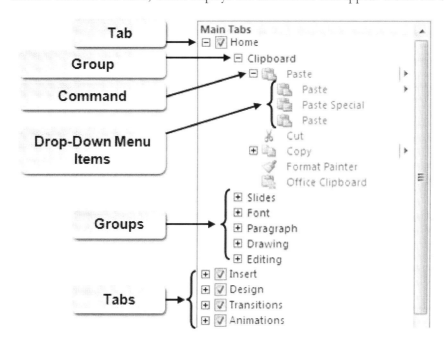

Figure 1-3: The tree hierarchy within the Customize the Ribbon pane.

The Customize Status Bar Menu

The **Customize Status Bar** menu allows you to select which status bar elements you want displayed. You can access the **Customize Status Bar** menu by right-clicking anywhere along the status bar.

The Customize Status Bar Menu

Note: As non-traditional computing devices such as tablet computers support an increasing number of applications, Logical Operations strives to produce courseware that is device agnostic. However, some commands in PowerPoint 2010 are not available directly on the user interface. In such cases, this course book will indicate the user should right-click, for example, to access a particular command. Please reference the user manual for your particular device for alternatives to the traditional mouse/keyboard commands.

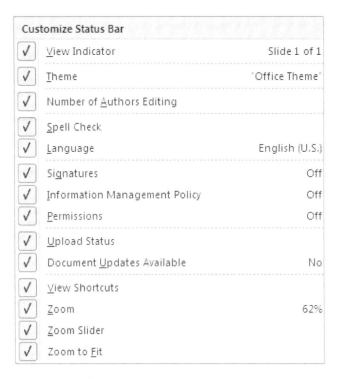

Figure 1–4: The Customize Status Bar menu.

 Access the Checklist tile on your LogicalCHOICE course screen for reference information and job aids on How to Customize the Ribbon and the Status Bar

ACTIVITY 1-1
Customizing the Ribbon and the Status Bar

Scenario

You are the communications director for Develetech Industries, a manufacturer of home electronics. Develetech is known as an innovative designer and producer of high-end televisions, video game consoles, laptop and tablet computers, and mobile phones.

Develetech is a mid-sized company, employing approximately 2,000 residents of Greene City and the surrounding area. Develetech also contracts with a number of offshore organizations for manufacturing and supply-chain support.

As the communications director, you are responsible for internal company communication and the release of public information such as press releases and employment opportunities. In a typical month, you are responsible for publication of the company newsletter, writing and distributing company-wide or departmental communications, updating the entries on Develetech's employment opportunity web page, responding to media requests for information, and distributing press releases regarding new Develetech products.

You frequently use PowerPoint 2010 to deliver important information both internally and externally. You are familiar with much of PowerPoint's functionality, but always strive to learn more in order to better develop professional, engaging, and visually captivating presentations. You have discovered several commands that you find useful, but that are not on the ribbon. You decide to create a tab to have easy access to these commands, and to have a place to add commands as you discover more of them. You have also noticed some "creative" names for themes built by some developers on your staff. They aren't inappropriate, but you feel they could distract people from the message in your department's communications. So, you decide to remove the theme name from the status bar.

1. Launch PowerPoint 2010.

2. Customize the status bar.
   a) Right-click the status bar.
   b) In the **Customize Status Bar** menu, deselect **Theme**.
   c) Click outside the **Customize Status Bar** menu to close it.
   d) Verify that the theme name no longer appears on the status bar.

3. Add a tab to the ribbon.
   a) Select **File→Options**, and then select **Customize Ribbon** in the **PowerPoint Options** dialog box.
   b) Select the **New Tab** button.
   c) Select **New Tab (Custom)** in the **Customize the Ribbon** pane, and then select **Rename**.
   d) In the **Rename** dialog box, type *Favorites* into the **Display name** field, and then select OK.

4. In the **Customize the Ribbon** pane, select the **Move Down** button until the **Favorites (Custom)** tab appears below the **View** tab to make the new tab the last tab on the ribbon.

5. Name the group in the **Favorites** tab.
   a) In the **Customize the Ribbon** pane, select **New Group (Custom)** from the **Favorites (Custom)** tab, and then select **Rename**.
   b) In the **Rename** dialog box, type *Favorite Commands* in the **Display** name field, and then select OK.

6. Add commands to the **Favorites** tab.
   a) Select the **Choose commands from** down-arrow, and then select **Commands Not in the Ribbon**.

   b) In the **Customize the Ribbon** pane, ensure that the **Favorite Commands (Custom)** group is still selected.

   c) Scroll down in the **Choose commands from** pane, select **Nudge Down**, and then select the **Add** button.

   d) Add the **Nudge Left**, **Nudge Right**, and **Nudge Up** commands to the **Favorite Commands (Custom)** group, and then select **OK**.

7. Select the **Favorites** tab, and then verify that the new commands are displayed in the **Favorite Commands** group.

The Window Group

PowerPoint 2010 allows you to work with multiple presentation windows at the same time. You can also create a duplicate version of an open presentation. This allows you to simultaneously view multiple slides from the same presentation in the Normal view. The **Window** group provides you with the commands to work with and display multiple presentation windows. You can access the **Window** group on the **View** tab.

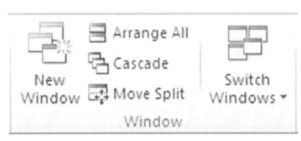

Figure 1–5: The Window group.

Window Group Command	Function
New Window	Creates a duplicate view of the presentation in a separate window. Once a duplicate view is created, the original presentation's file name will appear in the title bar with a ":1" after it. The duplicate view will appear with a ":2" after the file name in the title bar. This continues with subsequent open views.
Arrange All	Displays all open instances of PowerPoint 2010 on screen at the same time. Each open instance of PowerPoint 2010 receives roughly the same amount of screen space.
Cascade	Displays all open instances of PowerPoint 2010 in a diagonal, overlapping fashion. This allows you to view all of the presentation's title bars simultaneously.
Move Split	Moves the splitters that separate the various sections of the PowerPoint 2010 user interface, allowing you to customize the amount of screen space provided for the **Left** pane, the **Slide** pane, and the **Notes** pane. The **Move Split** button is active only when the presentation is in the Normal view.
Switch Windows	Allows you to select the open instance of PowerPoint 2010 that you wish to display on top of the others.

 Access the Checklist tile on your LogicalCHOICE course screen for reference information and job aids on How to Work with Multiple Windows Simultaneously

ACTIVITY 1-2
Working with Multiple Windows Simultaneously

Data Files

C:\091032Data\Modifying the PowerPoint Environment\Develetech press notification.pptx

C:\091032Data\Modifying the PowerPoint Environment\Develetech press notification_images added.pptx

Scenario

You are sending out a PowerPoint presentation to technology and computer magazines ahead of a press release for Develetech's new product line. Because you want as many media outlets as possible to cover the pending release, you'd like them to save the date. You asked a member of your team to add some content that was not originally in the PowerPoint file you are using for the communication. To make sure the content is in place before sending out the file, you will open the original file and the finished one so you can view them side by side to ensure the change was made.

1. Launch the presentation files.
   a) Open the C:\091032Data\Modifying the PowerPoint Environment\Develetech press notification.pptx file.
   b) Open the C:\091032Data\Modifying the PowerPoint Environment\Develetech press notification_images added.pptx file.

2. View the presentations side by side.
   a) Select **View→Window→Arrange All**.
   b) Review the presentations, verifying that the Develetech press notification_images added.pptx file contains the additional slide.

3. Close both of the presentations by selecting the **Close** buttons in the PowerPoint 2010 windows, leaving you with no open instances of the PowerPoint application.

Time permitting, you can encourage students to open further instances of PowerPoint 2010, perhaps by using the built-in templates, and to experiment with the various views from the **Window** group. Which do they find the most useful? Why?

TOPIC B

Set PowerPoint 2010 Options

It's happened to nearly everyone who has ever worked with a computer: You spend a lot of time working on a file, but forget to save your work. Suddenly, the power goes out, your computer crashes, or you encounter some other critical error. Lost work doesn't only mean lost time. Many times you're unable to recapture the essence of what you worked so hard to create. When these moments occur, all does not have to be lost.

In addition to providing you with the ability to modify the user interface, PowerPoint 2010 allows you to configure a multitude of options to control how the application behaves. PowerPoint can save files for you as you work, in whichever file format you choose, and place them wherever you would like them to be stored. And, your ability to configure PowerPoint goes well beyond file management. Understanding how to make PowerPoint work for you means you can focus on what's really important: delivering your message.

The Save Options

The Save Options

PowerPoint 2010 provides you with a number of Save options that you can configure to change how and where you save your files. You can also control how files are saved and merged when you and your colleagues work on a presentation simultaneously. The Save options are divided into four sections. You can access the Save options from the **Save** tab on the **PowerPoint Options** dialog box.

Save Option Section	Allows You To
Save Presentations	Determine the file format for saved presentations, and enable and configure **AutoRecover** settings.
Offline Editing Options for Document Management Server Files	Select a location to save files that you have checked out of a document management server to work on offline.
File Merge Options for Shared Document Management Server Files	Determine whether or not to review and accept changes from other authors working on a co-authored presentation before merging the changes with your document.
Preserve Fidelity When Sharing This Presentation	Embed fonts in a presentation file so they are available if the presentation is opened on a computer that doesn't have the fonts installed.

Advanced Options

The Advanced Options

PowerPoint 2010 provides you with many Advanced options, allowing you to optimize editing, printing, display, and other functionality to suit your needs. You can access the Advanced options from the **Advanced** tab on the **PowerPoint Options** dialog box. The Advanced options are divided into eight sections.

Advanced Option Section	Provides Options For
Editing Options	Selecting, dragging, and dropping text; and for setting the number of times an action can be undone.
Cut, Copy, and Paste	Displaying paste options when pasting, and for using smart cut and paste.

Advanced Option Section	Provides Options For
Image Size and Quality	Compressing images, setting default image resolution on output, and keeping or discarding editing data.
Display	Controlling the number of recent documents displayed, displaying particular on-screen elements, and determining the view in which presentations open.
Slide Show	Accessing menus and toolbars, and displaying annotations during a slide show.
Print	Determining printer resolution and aligning objects during printing.
When Printing This Document	Determining which print settings to use when printing a particular presentation.
General	Enabling add-in features, such as audio feedback and displaying user interface errors, and for accessing content shared online by other Microsoft Office users.

 Access the Checklist tile on your LogicalCHOICE course screen for reference information and job aids on How to Set PowerPoint 2010 Options

ACTIVITY 1–3
Setting PowerPoint 2010 Options

Scenario

Your team has had several recent incidents where work was lost because someone forgot to save their progress. This has caused some rework, which is hurting productivity. You have asked all members of your team to set PowerPoint to save AutoRecover files every five minutes. You decide to change this setting on your computer as well, and that this is a good opportunity to set some other options you've been meaning to change.

1. Launch PowerPoint 2010.

2. Set PowerPoint to save AutoRecover information every 5 minutes.
    a) If necessary, maximize the PowerPoint 2010 window.
    b) Select File→Options→Save.
    c) In the **PowerPoint Options** dialog box, in the **Save presentations** section, ensure the **Save AutoRecover information every** *X* **minutes** check box is checked.
    d) Use the spin buttons to set PowerPoint to save AutoRecover information every 5 minutes.

3. Set the maximum number of undos to 30.
    a) In the **PowerPoint Options** dialog box, select the **Advanced** tab.
    b) In the **Editing Options** section, use the spin buttons to set the value in the **Maximum number of undos** field to 30.

4. Change the number of recent documents PowerPoint displays in the **Backstage View**.
    a) In the **Display** section, select the text in the **Show this number of Recent Documents** field.
    b) Enter a value of *15* in the field, and then select OK.

Summary

In this lesson, you configured PowerPoint 2010 so you can work more quickly and efficiently in an environment tailor-made for you. You have the application working just the way you like it, and you have an understanding of how to adapt it as your needs change.

How can customizing the PowerPoint user interface improve your experience developing presentations?

A: Answers will vary, but may include accommodating personal habits and work flows, tailoring the application to a specific job function, and allowing for growth and variability as you begin to use more complex features of the application more frequently.

Based on your experience using other Microsoft Office applications, how do you feel about being able to work in multiple presentation windows at the same time? Is there as much of a need to do this in PowerPoint as with applications such as Word?

A: Answers will vary, but people who develop in PowerPoint frequently have likely experienced the frustration associated with saving, closing, and reopening files in order to move from presentation to presentation. Students may not feel they will use this feature as often in PowerPoint as in other applications, but most will likely see the value in having the ability to do so.

> **Note:** Check your LogicalCHOICE Course screen for opportunities to interact with your classmates, peers, and the larger LogicalCHOICE online community about the topics covered in this course or other topics you are interested in. From the Course screen you can also access available resources for a more continuous learning experience.

Remember to repeat in-class responses/ questions for remote students. Encourage all students to respond in the chat feature or on the whiteboard of your web conferencing system.

Encourage students to use the social networking tools provided on the LogicalCHOICE Home screen to follow up with their peers after the course is completed for further discussion and resources to support continued learning.

2 | Customizing Design Templates

Lesson Time: 45 minutes

Lesson Objectives

In this lesson, you will customize design templates. You will:

- Modify slide masters and slide layouts

- Add headers and footers

- Modify the notes master and the handout master

Lesson Introduction

Having worked with PowerPoint, you have likely experienced how templates and themes can help you create engaging, professional-looking presentations with a consistent look throughout. But, you may also have experienced the frustration of not having just the right template or theme available for a particular project. And, it's likely you have sat through numerous presentations that look just like all the others. So, how can you make your presentations stand out and work in every situation?

PowerPoint 2010 gives you the ability to not only customize any of the existing templates and themes, but it also allows you to create your own. Understanding how to create and modify design templates gives you complete control of the look and functionality of the slides in your presentations. This will save you the time and effort of searching for just the right template, which may not even exist. And, highly customized slides and printed materials will help your presentations stand out from the pack.

TOPIC A

Modify Slide Masters and Slide Layouts

It's frustrating to be unable to find just the right look or layout for your presentation. Equally frustrating is wasting time copying and pasting, or completely reformatting, slides each time you add one to your project. This can become especially difficult when large organizations need to create numerous presentations that all have a consistent look and feel.

PowerPoint 2010 allows you to customize the look of all of the slides in your presentation at once, saving you a lot of painstaking work. You can craft highly stylized layouts and templates that you can use throughout your presentation, and save for use in all presentations. Understanding just how quick and easy this is will go a long way to helping you create unique, stylish presentations that can be repurposed for a large number of users.

Slide Masters

Slide Masters

Ask the students if they can think of a reason for including two slide masters in the same presentation. One possibility: a presentation that compares and contrasts two different concepts—in compliance with policies versus in violation of policies.

Slide masters are elements of all PowerPoint 2010 presentations that determine the layout and thematic characteristics of all slides within a presentation. Slide masters determine the placement and formatting of text, and the layout of content on slides. Slide masters also define thematic elements, such as color schemes and effects. Changes you make to the slide master will affect all slides in the presentation that are based on the slide master. Presentations can contain more than one slide master. You can access slide masters in the **Master Views** group on the **View** tab.

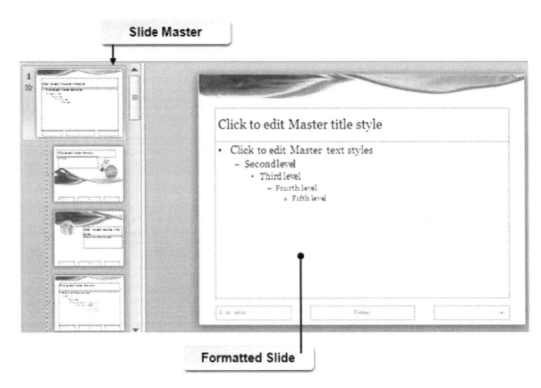

Figure 2-1: Slide masters define slide layouts and themes.

 Note: In the Slide Master view, slide master thumbnails appear above the slide layout thumbnails in the left pane. They are distinguishable from slide layouts as they appear as larger thumbnails.

The Slide Master Tab

The **Slide Master** tab is displayed to the left of the **Home** tab on the ribbon when you select the Slide Master view. The **Slide Master** tab contains functional groups of commands you will use to create, modify, and delete slide masters and slide layouts.

The Slide Master Tab

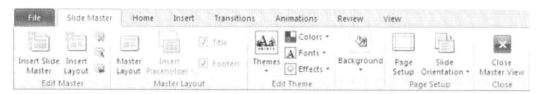

Figure 2-2: The Slide Master tab.

Slide Master Tab Group	Provides Commands To:
Edit Master	Create, name, and delete slide masters and slide layouts. The **Preserve** command in this group will save slide masters that you have added but have made no changes to.
Master Layout	Add or remove content placeholders, headers, and footers from slide layouts and slide masters.
Edit Theme	Apply thematic elements to slide masters and slide layouts.
Background	Format the background of slide masters and slide layouts.
Page Setup	Select the overall dimensions, aspect ratio, and orientation of slide masters, slide layouts, and printed materials.
Close	Close the Slide Master view.

Access the Checklist tile on your LogicalCHOICE course screen for reference information and job aids on How to Work with Slide Masters

ACTIVITY 2-1
Working with Slide Masters

Data Files

C:\091032Data\Customizing Design Templates\Develetech comms template.potx

C:\091032Data\Customizing Design Templates\Develetech_logo.png

Scenario

The VP of sales has asked that all internal communications directed to sales personnel have a different look than those for company-wide messaging. You decide to create a template for sales communications by modifying the slide master in the PowerPoint template you use for all other communications.

1. Open the C:\091032Data\Customizing Design Templates\Develetech comms template.potx file.

2. Select the slide master.
   a) Select View→Master Views→Slide Master.
   b) If necessary, select the slide master in the left pane.

3. Apply a new theme to the slide master.
   a) Select Edit Theme→Themes.
   b) Select the Concourse theme from the gallery.

    Note: The themes are listed in alphabetical order.

Check in with students to make sure they remember how to scale the image, as opposed to resizing it, using the options in the Format Picture dialog box. Check in with remote learners to ensure they are not falling behind.

Quiz the class to see if they know why the logo does not appear on all the slide layouts. The answer: The Hide Background Graphics check box is checked for some of the layouts.

4. Add the Develetech logo to the slide master.
   a) While in the Slide Master view, select Insert→Images→Picture.
   b) In the Insert Picture dialog box, navigate to the Develetech_logo.png file and select Insert.
   c) Scale down the Develetech_logo.png image by 50%.
   d) If necessary, display the rulers from the View tab.
   e) Select the title text placeholder and resize it by dragging the right sizing handle to the left until it is 2 inches right of center.
   f) Drag the Develetech_logo.png image to the top-right corner of the slide so that it occupies the space to the right of the title text placeholder.
   g) Verify that the Develetech logo appears in the same location on all of the applicable slide layouts in the left pane.
   h) Deselect the image.

5. Modify the background style of the slide master.
   a) Ensure that the Slide Master tab is selected, and then select Background→Background Styles.
   b) From the Background Styles gallery, select Style 5, which is the first style in the second row.
   c) Verify that the background style has been applied to all of the slide layouts in the left pane.

6. Save the newly formatted template as a presentation.
   a) Select File→Save As.
   b) In the Save As dialog box, if needed, navigate to the C:\091032Data\Customizing Design Templates folder, and then, in the File name field, type *My_Develetech sales comms presentation*.

c) In the **Save as type** field, ensure that **PowerPoint Presentation (*.pptx)** is selected, and then select **Save**.

Custom Slide Layouts

Having used PowerPoint 2010 for some time, you know that a slide layout determines the arrangement of content placeholders and/or on-screen elements on a slide. However, you may not have known that you can customize and create slide layouts to suit your needs.

Custom Slide Layouts

You can work with slide layouts in the **Slide Master** view. Slide layouts are displayed below their associated slide master in the left pane. The layouts that are displayed with the slide master are the layouts available when you add a slide from the **New Slide** drop-down menu in the **Slide** group on the **Home** tab. Any changes you make to the slide layouts in the **Slide Master** view, and any custom slides you create, are reflected in the **New Slide** drop-down menu. Typically, changes made to slide layouts in the **Slide Master** view affect only that particular layout. However, changes made to a slide layout in the **Edit Theme** group on the **Slide Master** tab will affect all slides associated with the same slide master.

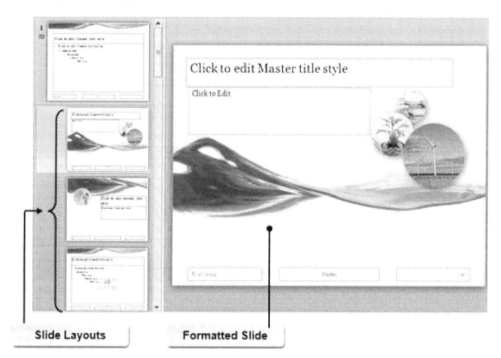

Figure 2-3: Slide layouts and their associated slide master.

Custom Themes

Custom themes are combinations of colors, fonts, and effects that you can define and apply to slides, slide masters, and slide layouts in PowerPoint. You can save custom themes for use in other presentations. Saved custom themes are displayed in the **Custom** section of the **Themes** gallery.

Custom Themes

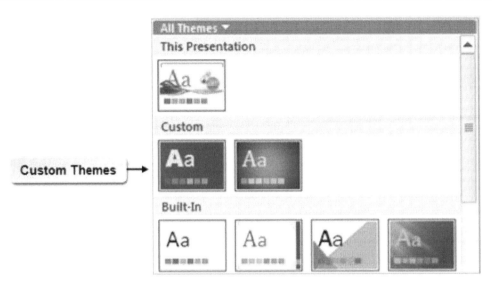

Figure 2–4: Custom themes in the Themes gallery.

 Access the Checklist tile on your LogicalCHOICE course screen for reference information and job aids on How to Customize Slide Layouts and Themes

ACTIVITY 2-2
Creating a Custom Slide Layout

Data File

C:\091032Data\Customizing Design Templates\microphone.jpg

Scenario

You have received a request from the Sales department to create a media slide layout for their presentation template. People in the department frequently include existing video content from the marketing department in their presentations. They feel it will save a lot of time to have an existing slide layout for them to use. They have also asked you to remove the title and footers placeholders, and to add a text placeholder for naming the source video.

The exact placement and sizing of on-screen objects is not important for this activity. Students can be creative if they so choose.

1. Insert a new slide layout.
   a) Ensure the presentation is still in the **Slide Master** view, and that the **Slide Master** tab is selected.
   b) Scroll to the bottom of the left pane and select the last slide layout in the presentation.
   c) In the **Edit Master** group, select **Insert Layout**.

2. Name the new slide layout.
   a) In the **Edit Master** group, select **Rename**.
   b) In the **Rename Layout** dialog box, in the **Layout name** field, delete the existing text, enter *Media Slide Layout* and then select **Rename**.

3. Remove the title and footers from the slide layout by deselecting the **Title** and **Footers** check boxes in the **Master Layout** group.

4. Add a media content placeholder to the slide layout.
   a) From the **Master Layout** group, select the **Insert Placeholder down-arrow**, and then select **Media**.
   b) Near the top-left corner of the slide layout, draw in a placeholder approximately 3 inches high by 4 inches wide.

Removing the background from an image is performed by selecting **Picture Tools contextual tab→Adjust→Remove Background**. Encourage students who remember how to use this feature to share their screens and demonstrate the procedure.

5. Add a text placeholder below the media content placeholder.
   a) Select the **Insert Placeholder** down-arrow, and then select **Text**.
   b) Draw the text placeholder below the media content placeholder.

6. Add an image to the slide layout.
   a) Select **Insert→Images→Picture**.
   b) Insert the C:\091032Data\Customizing Design Templates\microphone.jpg file.
   c) Scale down the image as you see fit, and then drag it to the right side of the slide layout.
   d) From the **Picture Tools** contextual tab, remove the plain white background from the image.

PowerPoint 2010 will sometimes default to the hidden Microsoft Templates folder when you save presentations as a template. Ensure the students are saving this template to the data files folder for this lesson.

7. Save the presentation as a template.
   a) Select **File→Save As**, and then, if necessary, navigate to the C:\091032Data\Customizing Design Templates folder.
   b) In the **Save As** dialog box, in the **File name** field, type *My_Develetech sales comms template*.
   c) In the **Save as type** field, select **PowerPoint Template (*.potx)**.
   d) Select **Save**.

8. Select **File→Close**.

TOPIC B

Add Headers and Footers

Typically, the content you include on the various slides in your presentations will be unique in some way. However, there are some types of information you may wish to include on all slides, or in all of your printed materials, such as the presentation date or page numbers. But manually numbering pages or entering the same information on all of the slides in your presentation is simply a waste of time.

PowerPoint 2010 gives you a number of options for automatically including such information on all of your slides or in your printed materials. By adding headers or footers to your presentation, you can automatically include important information where you need it without wasting effort performing repetitive tasks.

Footers and Headers

Headers and Footers

Encourage the students to think creatively about designing templates. Ask the students how they might be able to display "headers" on a slide. The answer: Include footers on the slides, but move them to the top of the slide layouts.

Footers are small content placeholders that can appear along the bottom of slides, handouts, and note pages. Footers can contain information such as the name of the presenter, the date of the presentation, or page numbers. You can also add images to footers and configure them as shapes.

Headers are similar to footers, except they appear along the top of the page. Headers can appear on printed materials such as handouts and notes pages, but they do not display on slides.

Although you can add headers and footers to individual slides and pages, you can also add them in the slide master or the layout masters to apply them to all slides or pages just like other template elements.

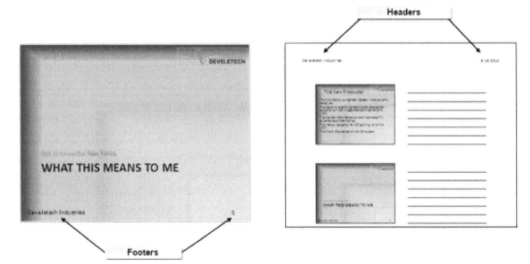

Figure 2–5: Footers can appear on all materials; headers do not appear on slides.

The Header and Footer Dialog Box

The Header and Footer Dialog Box

The **Header and Footer** dialog box provides you with various commands to add and configure headers and footers in your presentation. The commands are divided between two tabs: the **Slide** tab and the **Notes and Handouts** tab. The **Slide** tab allows you to add and configure footers only. The **Notes and Handouts** tab also includes commands for working with headers. You can access the **Header and Footer** dialog box from the **Text** group on the **Insert** tab.

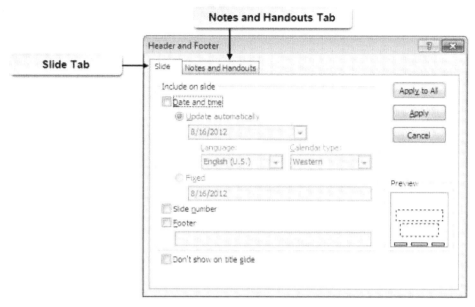

Figure 2–6: The tabs on the Header and Footer dialog box.

Access the Checklist tile on your LogicalCHOICE course screen for reference information and job aids on **How to Add Headers and Footers**

ACTIVITY 2-3
Adding Headers and Footers

Data File

C:\091032Data\Customizing Design Templates\Develetech comms template_with logo.potx

Scenario

To create more-professional-looking presentations and handouts, you decide to include headers and footers directly in the communications department's PowerPoint template. You feel this will help standardize the look of all presentations your team develops.

1. Open the C:\091032Data\Customizing Design Templates\Develetech comms template_with logo.potx file.

2. Add footers to the slides.
   a) Select View→Master Views→Slide Master.
   b) Select the slide master in the left pane.

    Note: Remember that the slide master is the top thumbnail in the left pane that is also larger than the thumbnails below it. Make sure that is what you are selecting and not one of the slide layouts.

   c) Select Insert→Text→Header & Footer.
   d) In the **Header and Footer** dialog box, ensure the **Slide** tab is selected.
   e) In the **Include on slide** section, check the **Slide number** check box.
   f) Check the **Footer** check box and, in the **Footer** field, type *Develetech Industries*.
   g) Check the **Don't show on title slide** check box and select **Apply to All**.
   h) In the slide pane, select the **date content placeholder** and press the **Delete** key.
   i) Drag the footer from the bottom center of the slide to the bottom-left corner of the slide.
   j) Select **Home→Paragraph→Align Text Left** ≡ .

3. Verify that the footer and slide number are displayed on the slides.
   a) Select **Slide Master→Close→Close Master View**.
   b) From the **Home** tab, add any type of slide other than a title slide.
   c) Verify that the footer and the slide number appear on the slide, and then delete the slide.

4. Add headers to the notes pages and other handouts.
   a) Select View→Master Views→Slide Master.
   b) Select the slide master in the left pane, and then select Insert→Text→Header & Footer.
   c) In the **Header and Footer** dialog box, select the **Notes and Handouts** tab.
   d) Check the **Date and time** check box, and then ensure the **Update automatically** radio button is selected.
   e) Check the **Header** check box and, in the **Header** field, type *Develetech Industries*.
   f) Ensure the **Page number** check box is checked, and then select **Apply to All**.
   g) Select **Slide Master→Close→Close Master View**.

5. Use **Print Preview** to verify the headers appear on printed materials.
   a) Select **File→Print**.

b) If necessary, select the button below the **Slides** field in the **Print** pane, and then select **Notes Pages** from the **Print Layout** section of the drop-down menu.

c) Verify that the header, date, and page number appear on the print preview in the right pane.

6. Save the file to the C:\091032Data\Customizing Design Templates folder as *My_Develetech comms template_with logo.potx*.

TOPIC C

Modify the Notes Master and the Handout Master

You may have particular needs when it comes to generating printed materials from your project. Organizations mindful of budgetary and environmental concerns may wish to use as little paper as possible when printing materials. Your audience may have a need for more space to take notes, or larger images for easier viewing. Whatever the reason, it would be far easier to make changes to all of the pages in your printed materials at once than to format each page manually.

The notes and handout masters in PowerPoint 2010 give you a similar level of control over your printed materials as slide layouts and slide masters give you over your slides. Taking a few moments to configure your printed materials ahead of time can pay off in saved time and effort, and by saving paper and its associated cost.

The Notes Master

The Notes Master

The *notes master* is to your notes pages what slide masters are to the slides in your presentation. Notes masters determine the placement, orientation, formatting, and styles of the content on your notes pages. You can access the notes master from the **Master Views** group on the **View** tab.

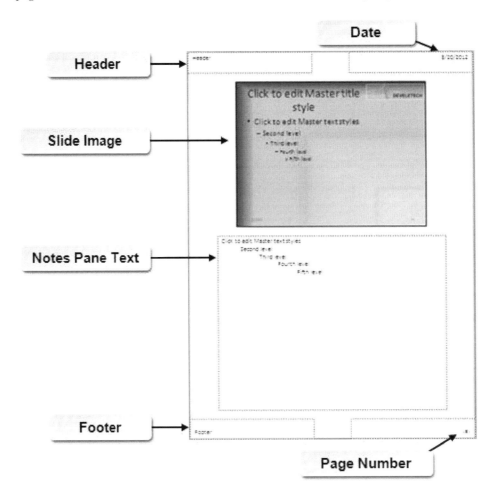

Figure 2-7: The notes master from a PowerPoint presentation.

The Handout Master

Much like the notes master does for your notes pages, the handout master determines the placement, formatting, and styles for the content on your handouts. You can also set the number of slides that are displayed per page in your handouts. You can access the handout master from the **Master Views** group on the **View** tab.

The Handout Master

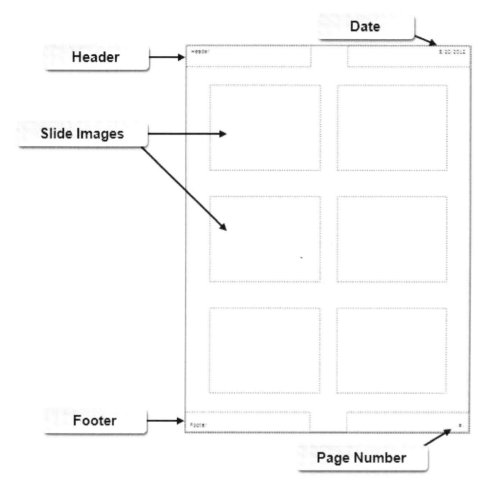

Figure 2-8: The handout master from a PowerPoint presentation.

 Access the Checklist tile on your LogicalCHOICE course screen for reference information and job aids on How to Modify Notes Masters and Handout Masters

ACTIVITY 2-4
Modifying Notes Masters and Handout Masters

Scenario

Several department heads have given you feedback regarding the printed materials they have had to generate from the presentations your department created. They consistently tell you that the notes pages are difficult to read for presenters, and that there are too many slides per page on the handouts for audience members to take notes. You decide to use the notes master and the handout master in your template to make global changes to all printed materials.

1. In the My_Develetech comms template_ with logo.potx file, select View→Master Views→Notes Master.

2. Decrease the size of the **slide image** on the notes pages.
   a) Select the **slide image** on the notes master, and then use the sizing handles to decrease its size.
   b) Using the gridlines and guides as necessary, center the slide image near the top of the notes master.

3. Increase the size of the notes text placeholder on the notes master by dragging the top-center sizing handle up until it is close to the slide image.

4. Increase the default size of notes text on the notes pages.
   a) Select all of the text in the notes text placeholder.
   b) Select **Home→Font→Font Size down-arrow.**
   c) Select **18** as the new font size.

5. Remove the footer text box from the notes master.
   a) Select the **Notes Master** tab.
   b) In the **Placeholders** group, uncheck the **Footer** check box.
   c) In the **Close** group, select **Close Master View**.

6. Change the default number of slides displayed per page from six to three.
   a) Select **View→Master Views→Handout Master**.
   b) In the **Page Setup** group, select **Slides Per Page**.
   c) Select **3 Slides** from the drop-down menu.

7. Remove the footer text box from the handout master by unchecking the **Footer** check box in the **Placeholders** group.

8. Close the **Handout Master** view, and then save and close the file.

Summary

In this lesson, you created design templates that will help you quickly and efficiently develop effective, high-impact presentations, notes pages, and handouts. PowerPoint is now performing a lot of the tedious groundwork involved in creating professional-looking presentations for you. This leaves you free to focus on crafting your message.

What are some potential pitfalls you may encounter when using templates to create your presentations?

A: Answers will vary, but relying on templates too much can make for repetitive presentations that lack originality. Although templates are great for quickly creating presentations that have a consistent look, the content is still the most important element of a great presentation.

What are some of the considerations that should go into creating an effective design template?

A: Answers will vary, but will likely include visual appeal, consistency with organizational branding, flexibility of use, and the ability to use the template for a long period of time without it seeming dated.

> **Note:** Check your LogicalCHOICE Course screen for opportunities to interact with your classmates, peers, and the larger LogicalCHOICE online community about the topics covered in this course or other topics you are interested in. From the Course screen you can also access available resources for a more continuous learning experience.

Call on a student you haven't heard from in a while. Proactively encourage remote students to respond. You can use the public chat or whiteboard features in your web conferencing system to collect responses, or have remote students respond via the video feed if it's available.

Encourage students to use the social networking tools provided on the LogicalCHOICE Home screen to follow up with their peers after the course is completed for further discussion and resources to support continued learning.

3 | Adding SmartArt to a Presentation

Lesson Time: 40 minutes

Lesson Objectives

In this lesson, you will add SmartArt to a presentation. You will:

- Create SmartArt

- Modify SmartArt

Lesson Introduction

Some information is best conveyed visually. Complex processes and high-level concepts are often difficult to communicate to an audience. You typically have a limited amount of time to conduct a presentation. As such, presenters have often relied on diagrams, flow charts, and other visual representations to make difficult subject matter clear and easy to digest in short periods of time. The down side of these visuals has traditionally been that they are difficult and time consuming to produce, often requiring the assistance of graphic designers.

PowerPoint 2010 includes a robust set of tools that make creating and modifying custom diagrams quick and easy. Becoming familiar with the on-board diagramming tools in PowerPoint will save you valuable development time, and free up precious time during your presentation by allowing you to simplify complex information.

TOPIC A

Create SmartArt

Creating complex graphical representations of textual information can be a daunting task. You must decide what shapes to include, how to size and format them, and how to arrange them on the slide so they make sense. You may know what you would like to communicate, but be unsure of how to say it visually. So, how do you go about designing and building your graphic? Luckily, you don't have to do all of the work yourself.

The SmartArt tools within PowerPoint 2010 give you a vast array of options for creating graphics that are well suited to a variety of needs. Understanding how to insert SmartArt into your presentations and how to decide which layout to use will save you countless hours of tedious formatting, not to mention a lot of frustration.

SmartArt Graphics

SmartArt Graphics

SmartArt graphics are visual representations of textual content that typically represent a process, a cycle, a hierarchy, or relationships. You can create SmartArt from existing text or build a graphic from scratch.

 Note: The individual elements of SmartArt graphics are known as shapes. This can be confusing as they share a name with the shapes you can add as a formattable text box. From this point on, the term *shapes* will refer to the shapes you can add as a text box, and the term *SmartArt shapes* will refer to the elements of a SmartArt graphic.

You may want to show LearnTO **Choose a SmartArt Layout** from the LogicalCHOICE Course screen or have students navigate out to the Course screen and watch it themselves as a supplement to your instruction. If not, please remind students to visit the LearnTOs for this course on their LogicalCHOICE Course screen after class for supplemental information and additional resources.

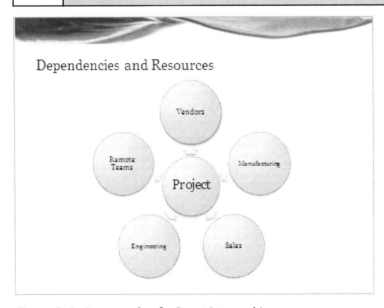

Figure 3-1: An example of a SmartArt graphic.

 Note: To further explore SmartArt, you can access the LearnTO **Choose a SmartArt Layout** presentation from the **LearnTO** tile on the LogicalCHOICE Course screen.

The Choose a SmartArt Graphic Dialog Box

The Choose a SmartArt Graphic Dialog Box

The **Choose a SmartArt Graphic** dialog box allows you to select from among the various categories and layouts of SmartArt to add to your presentation. The **Choose a SmartArt Graphic** dialog box also displays a preview and a description of the layout you select. You can access the **Choose a SmartArt Graphic** dialog box from the **Illustrations** group on the **Insert** tab.

The Text Pane

The **Text** pane allows you to add, remove, or edit text within your SmartArt graphics. You can display the **Text** pane whenever a SmartArt graphic is selected by using the control.

The Text Pane

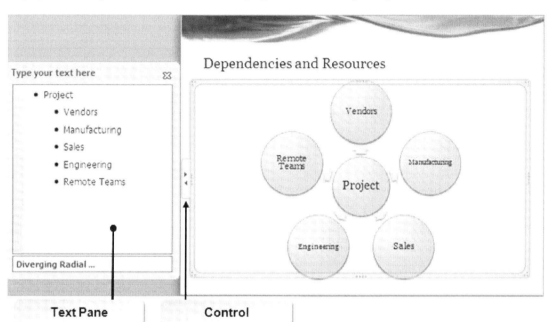

Figure 3-2: The Text pane allows you to work with text in a SmartArt graphic.

SmartArt Categories

There are eight categories of SmartArt graphics, each including a number of specific layouts, included with PowerPoint 2010. The particular layout you need to use is determined by the type of content you need to present. You can download additional SmartArt templates from Office.com.

SmartArt Category	Is Used to Create Diagrams for Displaying
List	Information that does not need to be shown in sequential order. Lists are ideal for content such as bulleted lists.
Process	Information that needs to be shown in sequential order, such as a process or procedure.
Cycle	A continuous process, such as an annual performance-review system or yearly sales cycles.
Hierarchy	Steps in a decision process or an organizational chart.
Relationship	How various elements of a system interconnect with each other.
Matrix	How various elements of a system relate to the system as a whole.
Pyramid	How elements of varying degrees of importance or size relate, proportionally, to each other as part of a whole.

SmartArt Category	Is Used to Create Diagrams for Displaying
Picture	Content as a combination of text and graphics.

 Access the Checklist tile on your LogicalCHOICE course screen for reference information and job aids on How to Add SmartArt to a Presentation

ACTIVITY 3-1
Adding SmartArt to a Presentation

Data File

C:\091032Data\Adding SmartArt to a Presentation\Develetech New Products Internal Release.pptx

Scenario

You are preparing an internal communications release to prepare all Develetech employees for the approaching new product release. As you reviewed the presentation, you noticed that one of the slides had a lot of text but no graphics. You want the communications release to be more energetic, so you decide to convert the text on that slide into SmartArt to liven up the presentation.

1. Launch the Develetech New Products Internal Release.pptx file.

2. Convert the text to a SmartArt graphic.
    a) Navigate to slide 4.
    b) Place the cursor anywhere inside the text box.
    c) Select **Home→Paragraph→Convert to SmartArt**.
    d) Select **Vertical Block List**, which is the second option in the top row, from the **SmartArt** gallery.

3. Add text to the SmartArt graphic.
    a) If necessary, select the control to display the **Text** pane.
    b) In the **Text** pane, place the cursor directly after the colon in the text placeholder for the "The Melius."
    c) Press the **Spacebar** once, and then type *a laptop that's* in the text placeholder.
    d) Add the word *and* before "smart for work."

4. Save the file to the C:\091032Data\Adding SmartArt to a Presentation folder as *My_Develetech New Products Internal Release.pptx*.

Check in with students as they convert the text to SmartArt. Encourage screen sharing for successes or challenges.

TOPIC B

Modify SmartArt

PowerPoint 2010 does a lot of the work for you when it comes to creating SmartArt graphics and converting text to SmartArt. However, you will likely find, from time to time, that you need to customize your SmartArt graphics to create the exact diagram you need.

PowerPoint 2010 gives you a high level of control over the formatting and style options that you can apply to the SmartArt graphics in your presentation. Understanding how to use these style and formatting options will give you the flexibility to create complex diagrams that look great and blend well with other elements in your presentation.

The SmartArt Tools Contextual Tab

The SmartArt Tools
Contextual Tab

The **SmartArt Tools** contextual tab displays the various commands you can use to create and modify SmartArt graphics. The **SmartArt Tools** contextual tab is divided into the **Design** and **Format** tabs.

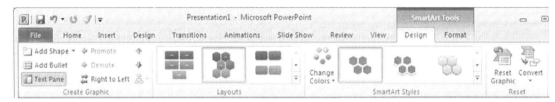

Figure 3-3: The SmartArt Tools contextual tab.

The Design Tab

The **Design** tab contains commands you can use to customize the overall look of your SmartArt graphics. The **Design** tab is divided into four functional groups.

Design Tab Group	Contains Commands For
Create Graphic	Adding shapes and text to SmartArt graphics, and arranging the order of SmartArt shapes.
Layouts	Selecting or modifying the layout of your SmartArt graphic.
SmartArt Styles	Applying effects to and modifying the color scheme of SmartArt graphics.
Reset	Discarding all formatting changes to SmartArt graphics, and converting SmartArt graphics to shapes or text.

The Format Tab

The **Format** tab contains commands you will use to modify the structure of your SmartArt graphics, as well as certain formatting and style commands. The **Format** tab is divided into five functional groups.

Format Tab Group	Contains Commands For
Shapes	Changing the shape or the size or SmartArt shapes, and temporarily converting 3-D SmartArt graphics to 2-D for editing purposes.

Format Tab Group	Contains Commands For
Shape Styles	Modifying fills, outlines, and effects for SmartArt shapes.
WordArt Styles	Applying or modifying WordArt styles to text in SmartArt graphics.
Arrange	Placing SmartArt graphics in front of or behind other on-screen objects.
Size	Scaling or resizing SmartArt graphics.

The Selection and Visibility Pane

Arranging objects on your slides can be a bit tricky, especially when you have many on-screen elements that overlap in multiple locations on your slides. The *Selection and Visibility pane* allows you to view the order in which objects appear on your slides and rearrange those objects quickly and easily.

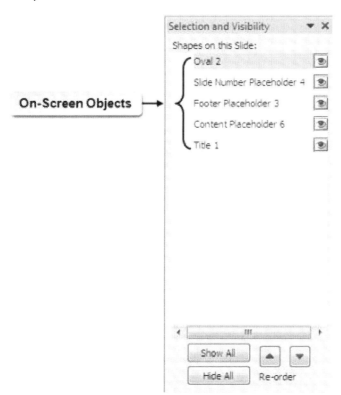

Figure 3–4: Objects displayed on the Selection and Visibility pane.

The Selection and Visibility Pane

Ask the students to discuss a time they may have struggled to arrange objects on screen. Would the **Selection and Visibility** pane have been helpful? Encourage remote students to respond via chat or the whiteboard if such tools are available.

 Access the Checklist tile on your LogicalCHOICE course screen for reference information and job aids on How to Modify SmartArt

ACTIVITY 3-2
Modifying SmartArt

Scenario

You prefer the SmartArt graphic over the plain text for your PowerPoint slide, but you feel it is too plain looking, and that it doesn't blend well with the rest of the presentation. You decide to format the SmartArt graphic for greater consistency and visual appeal.

1. Ensure that the SmartArt graphic is selected and the **Text** pane is displayed.

2. Demote the product descriptions in the SmartArt graphics's hierarchy so that they appear in separate SmartArt shapes.

   a) Place the insertion point directly before the word "our" in the first bullet point in the **Text** pane, and then press the **Enter** key.

   b) On the **SmartArt Tools** contextual tab, select **Design→Create Graphic→Demote**.

   c) Capitalize the "O" in "our," and remove the colon after "The Knomatico."

   d) Repeat the procedure for the remaining products.

   e) Close the **Text** pane.

    Note: Most text editing can be performed in either the **Text** pane or directly in the SmartArt graphic.

3. Modify the layout of the SmartArt graphic.

   a) In the **Layouts** group, select the **More** button on the **Layouts** gallery.

   b) Select **Grouped List** from the gallery.

4. Modify the style of the SmartArt graphic.

   a) In the **SmartArt Styles** group, select the **More** button on the **SmartArt Styles** gallery.

   b) From the 3-D section, select the **Polished** style, which is the first style in that section of the gallery.

   c) Select the **Change Colors** button to display the **Change Colors** gallery.

   d) Scroll down to the **Accent 6** section, and then select **Colored Outline - Accent 6**, which is the first color scheme in the section.

5. Save and close the presentation.

Students do not necessarily have to follow this procedure exactly as it is outlined in the activity. Encourage students to be creative with formatting the SmartArt graphic.

Encourage local and remote students to share interesting designs they may have created.

Summary

In this lesson, you created SmartArt graphics to visually convey textual information to your audience. You can now create an incredible array of graphics and illustrations for a wide range of purposes.

What impact will the ability to use SmartArt graphics have on your presentation designs?

A: Answers will vary, but students will likely gravitate away from excessive use of simple text, given the ease of creating SmartArt graphics.

What organizational benefits are there to having this level of functionality available in PowerPoint?

A: Answers will vary, but one of the greatest benefits is that this frees up the time of graphic and visual designers, who no longer have to frequently create graphics for presentations. The person who is developing the presentation also benefits from not having to wait on, or work around the schedule of, graphic artists.

Check in with and encourage remote students to participate in the discussion. Proactively call on students you haven't heard from lately.

 Note: Check your LogicalCHOICE Course screen for opportunities to interact with your classmates, peers, and the larger LogicalCHOICE online community about the topics covered in this course or other topics you are interested in. From the Course screen you can also access available resources for a more continuous learning experience.

Encourage students to use the social networking tools provided on the LogicalCHOICE Home screen to follow up with their peers after the course is completed for further discussion and resources to support continued learning.

4 | Working with Media and Animations

Lesson Time: 1 hour, 15 minutes

Lesson Objectives

In this lesson, you will work with media and animations. You will:

- Add audio to a presentation
- Add video to a presentation
- Customize animations and transitions

Lesson Introduction

Multimedia content surrounds us almost constantly. Today, people are accustomed to receiving messages in multiple formats, on numerous devices, in nearly any location, all day long. To an extent, this has increased the expectation among audiences for some type of sophisticated, multimedia experience during presentations. Many organizations are happy to accommodate this expectation. This means you may often be called upon to add audio, video, and other media content to your presentations.

Whether or not you feel media files are the best means of conveying a particular piece of information, you have been asked to include them in your presentation, or you simply wish to add a bit of excitement for the audience, understanding how to incorporate sound, video, and complex animations can help you create high-impact, dynamic presentations. PowerPoint 2010 provides you with robust capabilities for adding, editing, and customizing audio, video, and animations.

TOPIC A

Add Audio to a Presentation

Audio is an often-overlooked element of PowerPoint presentations. Although it should be used sparingly and tastefully, audio can enhance your content and set the mood or tone for your presentation. Sound effects are a good way of emphasizing key points. You may wish to add walk-in music to avoid an uncomfortable silence while audience members file into the venue and take their seats. Or, someone who would like to speak at your event may be unavailable; adding a recorded message to the presentation allows that person to participate even though he or she isn't present.

PowerPoint 2010 allows you to insert sound to your presentation from files on your computer and from the **Clip Art** gallery. You can also record audio directly to your slides. Understanding how to incorporate audio from various sources into your slides gives you a wide array of options for adding energy and impact to your presentations.

Audio File Formats

PowerPoint 2010 supports a number of audio file formats for use in your presentations.

Audio File Format	File Extension	Description
AIFF	.aiff	Audio file format originally used on Apple and SGI computers. These are mono audio files, but are uncompressed, which can result in large files.
AU Audio File	.au	Audio file format typically used for UNIX computers or web-based audio.
MIDI File	.mid or .midi	The standard format for sharing musical information between electronic instruments and computers.
MP3 Audio File	.mp3	Compressed audio file that is typically used for consumer audio storage and playback.
Windows Audio File	.wav	A typically uncompressed audio file that is the main format used in Microsoft Windows. This is also the format typically used for music CDs.
Windows Media Audio File	.wma	Compressed audio file that is typically used to distribute music files over the Internet.

The Audio/Video Controls

The Audio/Video
Controls

When you add an audio or a video clip to a slide in PowerPoint, the audio/video controls are displayed below the sound icon or the video window. During a slide show, you can play audio and video files by using the audio/video controls, or you can automate playback.

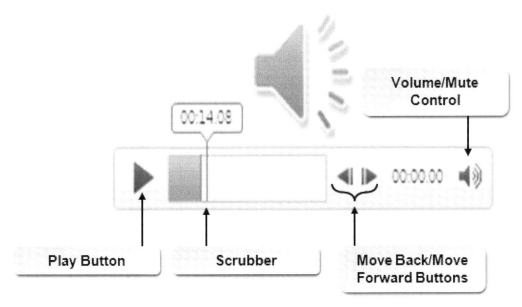

Figure 4-1: The audio/video controls displayed below the sound icon.

Bookmarks

Bookmarks are graphical markers that you can insert into the timeline of an audio or video clip. You can use bookmarks to quickly locate an important part of an audio or video clip from which to begin playback. You can also use them as guides for trimming audio and video clips to particular start and end points, or for triggering animations.

 Note: Using bookmarks to trigger animations will be covered in Topic C of this lesson.

The Audio Tools Contextual Tab

The **Audio Tools** contextual tab contains the commands you will use to work with audio files on your slides. The **Audio Tools** contextual tab is displayed when you insert or select an audio file. It is divided into two tabs: the **Format** tab and the **Playback** tab. The **Format** tab contains all of the commands you will use to control how the audio file appears on the slide. These commands are identical to those used to format pictures. The **Playback** tab contains the commands you will use to edit and preview the actual audio file.

Figure 4-2: The Audio Tools contextual tab.

The Playback Tab

You can edit your audio files and set audio options on the **Playback** tab. The **Playback** tab is divided into four groups.

Bookmarks

This is a good opportunity to ask the students if they can think of other uses for the bookmarks feature. One possibility: to flag a piece of audio or video for content review/approval. Encourage remote students to respond via chat or the video link.

The Audio Tools Contextual Tab

The Playback Tab

Playback Tab Group	Provides Commands For
Preview	Previewing your audio files and edits.
Bookmarks	Adding bookmarks to your audio file for playing back files from a particular point on the timeline.
Editing	Trimming sections of audio from the file and adding fades.
Audio Options	Adjusting the volume of your audio file and configuring playback options.

The Trim Audio Dialog Box

The Trim Audio Dialog Box

The **Trim Audio** dialog box allows you to set the start and end points of audio files to play back only the audio you wish to include in your presentation. You can access the **Trim Audio** dialog box from the **Editing** group on the **Playback** tab.

 Note: While you cannot add or remove bookmarks in the **Trim Audio** dialog box, they do appear in the dialog box's timeline. You can use bookmarks as graphical cues for setting start and end points.

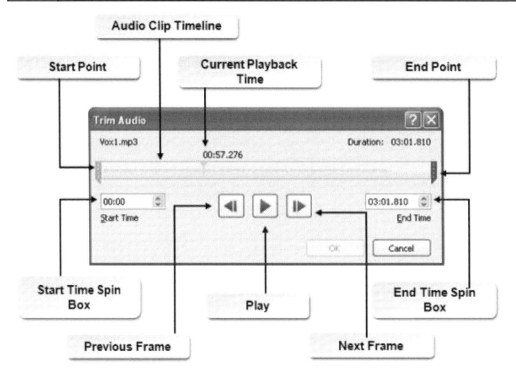

Figure 4–3: The Trim Audio dialog box.

 Note: The functionality of the **Trim Video** dialog box is nearly identical to that of the **Trim Audio** dialog box.

Trim Audio Dialog Box Element	Function
Audio Timeline	Displays a graphical representation of the time duration of the audio file.
Start Point	Displays and allows you to modify the current start point for the audio file graphically.

Trim Audio Dialog Box Element	Function
End Point	Displays and allows you to modify the current end point for the audio file graphically.
Current Playback Point	Displays the current playback point for previewing the audio file in the **Trim Audio** dialog box.
Start Time spin box	Displays and allows you to modify the current start point for the audio file numerically.
End Time spin box	Displays and allows you to modify the current end point for the audio file numerically.
Previous Frame button	Moves the current playback point back 0.1 seconds. (For video, it moves back one frame.)
Play button	Plays a preview of the audio clip from the current playback point. This button becomes the **Pause** button while the audio clip is playing.
Next Frame button	Moves the current playback point forward 0.1 seconds. (For video, it moves forward one frame.)

 Access the Checklist tile on your LogicalCHOICE course screen for reference information and job aids on How to Add, Edit, and Play Audio

ACTIVITY 4-1
Adding Audio to a Presentation

Data Files

C:\091032Data\Working with Media and Animations\Develetech New Products Internal Release_with SmartArt.pptx

C:\091032Data\Working with Media and Animations\celebrate.wav

Scenario

You feel the internal release presentation looks much better with the SmartArt graphic you created, but you also think it could use a bit more energy. You decide to add some upbeat music to the final slide to pump up the audience at the end of the presentation.

Ask students to turn down the volume on their computers for this activity. This is especially important if you have remote students. Playing back audio at a high volume level can cause feedback in your audio feed. Headphones or earbuds may also be helpful depending on your audio setup.

1. Launch the C:\091032Data\Working with Media and Animations\Develetech New Products Internal Release_with SmartArt.pptx file.

2. Insert an audio file.
   a) Navigate to the last slide.
   b) Select Insert→Media→Audio.
   c) In the Insert Audio dialog box, navigate to the C:\091032Data\Working with Media and Animations \celebrate.wav file, and select Insert.

3. Edit the audio clip.
   a) On the Audio Tools contextual tab, select Playback→Editing→Trim Audio.
   b) Drag the end point or use the spin buttons in the End Time field to trim the audio file to end at exactly 00:49, and then select OK.
   c) In the Editing group, use the spin buttons in the Fade Out field to add a 00.50 second fade out at the end of the audio file.

4. Lower the volume of the audio clip by selecting Audio Options→Volume, and then selecting Medium from the drop-down menu.

5. Set the audio file to play automatically when the slide is displays by selecting the down-arrow in the Start field, and then selecting Automatically from the drop-down menu.
   a) In the Start field, select the down-arrow.
   b) From the drop-down menu, select Automatically.

6. Check the Hide During Show check box to hide the audio controls during the slide show.

7. Preview the slide.
   a) Select Slide Show→Start Slide Show→From Current Slide.
   b) Press the Esc key to end the slide show after the audio clip plays.

8. Save the file to the C:\091032Data\Working with Media and Animations folder as *My_Develetech New Products Internal Release_with SmartArt.pptx*.

TOPIC B

Add Video to a Presentation

The proliferation of digital video content has made it increasingly easy to produce, edit, store, and share video. As a result, there is a growing demand for the use of video during presentations of all stripes. And, there is an ever-growing supply of content, for all sorts of applications, at your disposal. It is, indeed, likely that you will either want or be asked to include video content in a presentation at some point in time.

The video functionality available in PowerPoint 2010 gives you the ability to include existing content in your presentations, and to edit it for your exact needs. Becoming familiar with how to insert and modify video content in your presentations will allow you to leverage existing content, saving you the effort of recreating a slide-based version of the same content. PowerPoint 2010 also gives you the ability to embed web-based video in your presentations, opening the door for a massive array of options to make your presentations engaging, informative, and versatile.

Video File Formats

PowerPoint 2010 supports a number of video file formats you can add to your presentations.

Video File Format	File Extension	Description
Adobe® Flash Media	.swf	Format used to distribute web-based video using the Adobe Flash Player.
Windows Media File	.asf	Format used for streaming audio, video, images, and script commands across a network.
Windows Video File	.avi	Popular audio and video file format that can store content that has been compressed using a wide variety of codecs.
Movie File	.mpg or .mpeg	Format typically used for Video-CD and CD-i media.
Windows Media Video File	.wmv	Highly compressed audio and video file format that uses a minimal amount of storage.

The Video Tools Contextual Tab

The **Video Tools** contextual tab is displayed when you insert or select a video file in your presentation. The **Video Tools** contextual tab contains all of the commands you will use to work with video files on your slides. It is divided into two tabs: the **Format** tab and the **Playback** tab.

The Video Tools Contextual Tab

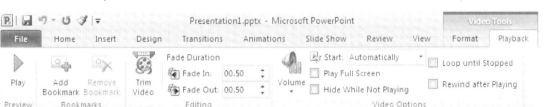

Figure 4–4: The Video Tools contextual tab.

The Format Tab

The **Format** tab contains all of the commands you will use to control how the video file appears on your slides. It is divided into five groups.

Format Tab Group	Provides Commands For
Preview	Previewing the video file and applied formatting.
Adjust	Selecting the preview image for the video window, applying color corrections to the video file, and adjusting the brightness and contrast of the video file.
Video Styles	Modifying the shape and style of the video border, and applying video effects to the video file.
Arrange	Reordering video files and other on-slide objects in your presentations.
Size	Cropping and resizing the video window.

Poster Frames

Poster Frames

Ask the students where they commonly encounter examples of poster frames. This can help provide real-world examples to demonstrate the concept. Common responses could include: the video section of a news web site, or preview images on sites such as YouTube.

Poster frames are the preview images that are displayed for videos in a presentation. The poster frame appears in the video player before the video plays. You can set a frame from the video clip as the poster frame, or you can insert an existing image file.

 Access the Checklist tile on your LogicalCHOICE course screen for reference information and job aids on How to Add and Format Video

ACTIVITY 4-2
Adding Video to a Presentation

Data File

C:\091032Data\Working with Media and Animations\Develetech new products promo.wmv

Scenario

A colleague of yours recommended including a video produced by the marketing team in the new product release presentation. You feel it would add further excitement to the presentation, and agree it should be included. You create a slide to display the video following the slide that introduces the new products.

1. Insert the video file.
   a) Navigate to slide 3, and then insert a new blank slide.
   b) Select **Insert→Media→Video**.
   c) In the **Insert Video** dialog box, navigate to the C:\091032Data\Working with Media and Animations \Develetech new products promo.wmv file, and then select **Insert**.
   d) If necessary, use the sizing handles to resize the video, and then use the guides to center the video on the slide.

2. Set a frame as the poster frame for the video.
   a) Use the video controls or click along the video timeline to place the scrubber at the desired frame of video. (The Develetech logo appears at about 6:00.)
   b) In the **Video Tools** contextual tab, select **Format→Adjust→Poster Frame**, and then select **Current Frame** from the drop-down menu.

3. Add a video style to the video.
   a) In the **Video Styles** group, select the **More** button to display the **Video Styles** gallery.
   b) From the **Intense** section, select **Beveled Rounded Rectangle**, which is the second style in the top row.

4. Select **Preview→Play** to view the video clip.

5. Save the file.

Ask students to turn down the volume on their computers for this activity. This is especially important if you have remote students. Playing back audio at a high volume level can cause feedback in your audio feed. Headphones or earbuds may also be helpful depending on your audio setup.

The Playback Tab

The **Playback** tab contains the commands you will use to edit video, and to set playback options for video during slide shows. It is divided into four groups.

The Playback Tab

Playback Tab Group	Provides Commands For
Preview	Previewing your video files and edits.
Bookmarks	Adding bookmarks to your video files for playing back files from a particular point on the timeline.
Editing	Trimming sections of video from the file and adding fades.

Playback Tab Group	Provides Commands For
Video Options	Adjusting the volume of your video file and configuring playback options.

 Access the Checklist tile on your LogicalCHOICE course screen for reference information and job aids on How to Edit and Play Video

ACTIVITY 4-3
Setting Video Playback Options

Scenario

You realize you will need to adjust some of the playback setting for the video file in order for it to play the way you would like. Also, you noticed there is a lot of blank space at the beginning and the end of the clip, so you decide to trim the ends of the video and add fades at the beginning and at the end.

1. Set the playback settings for the video.
   a) If necessary, select the video and, in the **Video Tools** contextual tab, access the **Playback** tab.
   b) Select **Volume**, and then select **Medium** from the drop-down menu.
   c) In the **Video Options** group, select the down arrow in the **Start** field, and then select **Automatically** from the drop-down menu.
   d) Check the **Rewind after Playing** check box.

2. Trim the beginning and the end of the clip to eliminate the blank spaces.
   a) In the **Editing** group, select **Trim Video**.
   b) In the **Trim Video** dialog box, drag the start and end points or use the spin buttons in the **Start Time** and **End Time** fields to trim out the blank spaces at the beginning and the end of the video, leaving about 2 seconds of blank space just before and just after the video.
   c) Select **OK**.

3. Add a 0.5 second fade at the beginning and at the end of the video by setting the **Fade In** and **Fade Out** fields to 00.50.

4. In the **Preview** section, select **Play** to preview the video.

5. Save the presentation.

Ask students to turn down the volume on their computers for this activity. This is especially important if you have remote students. Playing back audio at a high volume level can cause feedback in your audio feed. Headphones or earbuds may also be helpful depending on your audio setup.

TOPIC C

Customize Animations and Transitions

Graphics, tables, and charts can help you convey your message and keep your presentation engaging. Sometimes you need more energy or emphasis at certain points in your presentation. Animations and transitions can add energy and excitement to a presentation.

PowerPoint 2010 gives you the ability to create highly customized animations to create just the right effect. And you can use animation and transitions to automate the progression of your slide shows. By customizing your animations and transitions, you can highlight key points, energize your audience, and tailor the delivery of your presentation to suit virtually any situation.

The Animation Pane

The Animation Pane

The **Animation** pane allows you to reorder, set the timing of, configure, and remove animations on the slides in your presentation. You cannot add animations to objects in the **Animation** pane. You can access the **Animation** pane from the **Advanced Animation** group on the **Animations** tab.

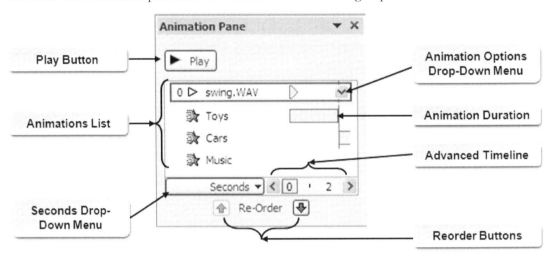

Figure 4-5: The Animation pane allows you to simultaneously manage all animations on a slide.

Animations Pane Element	Allows You To
Play button	Preview the animations on the selected slide.
Animations list	View the order of the animations on a slide, and set animation options for each of the animations.
Advanced Timeline	View the playback timeline of the animations on the selected slide.
Seconds drop-down menu	Zoom in or out of the **Advanced Timeline** view.
Reorder buttons	Change the order in which animations will occur on the slide during a slide show.
Animation Options drop-down menu	Change options like how the animation starts and showing/hiding the **Advanced Timeline**.

The Effect Options Dialog Box

The **Effect Options** dialog box gives you access to the commands you can use to customize the animations in your presentation. The **Effect Options** dialog box displays the name of the selected animation effect in the title bar. There are typically two or three tabs within the **Effect Options** dialog box, which include the **Effect** tab, the **Timing** tab, and the **Text Animation** tab. You can access the **Effects Options** dialog box from the drop-down arrow of the selected animation effect in the **Animation** pane.

The Effect Options
Dialog Box

 Note: The **Text Animation** tab appears only when certain objects that can contain text, such as shapes, are selected. The **Text Animation** tab does not, however, appear when text boxes are selected.

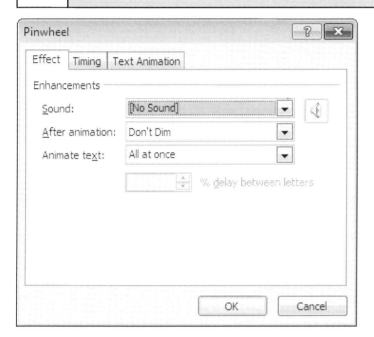

Figure 4–6: The Effect Options dialog box for the Pinwheel effect.

Effect Options Dialog Box Tab	Contains Commands For
Effect	Adding enhancements to an effect, such as including sound effects, changing the object's appearance after the effect plays, and animating text by letter, word, or all at once.
Timing	Starting, delaying, timing, and repeating animation effects.
Text Animation	Animating text by paragraph, including the text-containing shape in the animation, and animating text in reverse order.

 Access the Checklist tile on your LogicalCHOICE course screen for reference information and job aids on How to Customize Animations

ACTIVITY 4-4
Creating Custom Animation Effects

Scenario

After adding the audio and video files to the presentation, you feel the static images of the new products on slide 3 are too dull. You decide to add animation to the images to begin building the presentation's energy even before the video plays.

Ask students to turn down the volume on their computers for this activity. This is especially important if you have remote students. Playing back audio at a high volume level can cause feedback in your audio feed.

1. Navigate to slide 3.

2. Apply an animation effect to a graphic.
    a) Select the image of the laptop computer, and then access the **Animations** tab.
    b) In the **Animation** group, select the **More** button on the **Animation** gallery, and then select **More Entrance Effects**.
    c) In the **Change Entrance Effect** dialog box, in the **Moderate** section, select **Basic Zoom**, and then select **OK**.

3. Modify the animation effect.
    a) Select the **Effect Options** button.
    b) Select **In From Screen Center** from the drop-down menu.

4. Add a sound effect to the animation.
    a) Select the **dialog box launcher** in the **Animation** group.
    b) In the **Basic Zoom** dialog box, ensure the **Effect** tab is selected.
    c) In the **Enhancements** section, select the down-arrow on the **Sound** field, and then select **Push**.
    d) Select **OK**.

5. Adjust the animation effect timing.
    a) In the **Animation** group, select the **dialog box launcher**.
    b) In the **Basic Zoom** dialog box, select the **Timing** tab.
    c) Select the text in the **Duration** field, and then type *2.25*.

6. Set the animation effect to automatically play when the slide is displayed.
    a) Select the down-arrow in the **Start** field.
    b) Select **After Previous** in the drop-down menu, and then select **OK**.

7. Apply the effect to the remaining graphics on the slide.
    a) Select the image of the laptop computer, and then double-click **Animation Painter** in the **Advanced Animation** group to activate sticky mode.

     Note: If you click anywhere outside of the objects on your slide, you will deactivate sticky mode.

    b) Select the remaining graphics in the following order to apply the animation effect to each: the mobile phone, the tablet computer, the television, and the video game console.
    c) Select **Animation Painter** to deactivate sticky mode.

8. Preview the animation effects by selecting **Preview** in the **Preview** group.

9. Alter the order of the animations.

a) In the **Advanced Animation** group, select **Animation Pane**.

b) Select **Picture 8** in the **Animation** pane, and then select the **Down Arrow Re-Order** button.

c) Close the **Animation** pane.

10. Preview the animation effects to verify that the order has changed, and then save the presentation.

The Timing Group

As with animations, you can manually trigger the transitions in your presentation, or set them to advance automatically. The **Timing** group on the **Transitions** tab contains the commands you can use to control the timing of your slide transitions during a slide show.

The Timing Group

 Access the Checklist tile on your LogicalCHOICE course screen for reference information and job aids on How to Time Slide Transitions

ACTIVITY 4-5
Timing Slide Transitions

Scenario

As you are emailing the New Product Launch presentation to Develetech employees to view on their own, you decide to time some of the slides to play automatically when they view the slide show. Because there is not a lot of text to read until after the video on slide 4, you decide to time the first four slides to advance automatically.

1. Navigate to slide 1.

2. Apply a transition to the slide.
   a) Access the **Transitions** tab.
   b) In the **Transition to This Slide** group, select **Push** from the **Transitions** gallery.

3. Adjust the transition timing.
   a) In the **Timing** group, use the spin buttons in the **Duration** field to set the transition duration to 1.25 seconds.
   b) In the **Advance Slide** section, uncheck the **On Mouse Click** check box.
   c) Check the **After** check box, and then use the spin buttons to set the transition timing to 3.00 seconds.

4. Repeat steps 2 and 3 for slides 2 and 3.

5. Navigate to slide 4, and then apply the **Push** transition with the same timing as the previous slides. However, leave slide 4 set to advance on mouse click.

6. Preview the slide show through slide 4.
   a) Select **Slide Show→Start Slide Show→From Beginning**.
   b) View the first four slides of the slide show.
   c) Press the **Esc** key to end the slide show.

7. Save the presentation, and then close the file.

Summary

In this lesson, you worked with media and animations to craft an exciting and engaging presentation that uses a host of existing resources, and displays exactly as you'll need it to during an event. You can now develop highly sophisticated, versatile presentations that will keep the audience focused on your message.

How does including multimedia content in presentations benefit the audience? The presenter?

A: Answers will vary, but will likely include making the presentation far more engaging to the audience, and allowing for the inclusion of relevant, existing content. Presenter benefits include the ability to leverage nearly limitless content, and the ability to take a break during the presentation to regroup, organize thoughts, or set up for another segment of the presentation without losing the audience's focus.

What are some potential pitfalls to consider when timing animations and transitions?

A: Answers will vary, but could include not being able to account for unexpected delays, interruptions, or questions during a live event if the presenter is not immediately able to drive the slide show.

Encourage remote students to participate in the discussion. Check in with students you haven't heard from in a while.

 Note: Check your LogicalCHOICE Course screen for opportunities to interact with your classmates, peers, and the larger LogicalCHOICE online community about the topics covered in this course or other topics you are interested in. From the Course screen you can also access available resources for a more continuous learning experience.

Encourage students to use the social networking tools provided on the LogicalCHOICE Home screen to follow up with their peers after the course is completed for further discussion and resources to support continued learning.

5 | Collaborating on a Presentation

Lesson Time: 1 hour, 10 minutes

Lesson Objectives

In this lesson, you will collaborate on a presentation. You will:

- Review a presentation
- Publish and reuse slides
- Share a presentation on the web

Lesson Introduction

Very little work gets done by just one person anymore. Collaboration is a key component of nearly all work-related tasks, and teamwork is necessary to accomplish most goals. But involving greater numbers of people on particular projects or tasks requires greater amounts of communication and organization. Too many people working on the same file or document can lead to outdated versions, missing content, missed feedback, and general disorganization. And, all of that leads to poor quality, low morale, and high costs. You need a way to keep the traffic in check as multiple people contribute to the same project.

PowerPoint 2010 contains robust functionality to help you manage the collaboration that will lead to top-notch presentations. Taking control of the activity surrounding your presentations will help keep your team on track, ensure everyone's contributions are included, and help everyone involved avoid unnecessary or redundant work.

TOPIC A

Review a Presentation

One of the key aspects of collaborating on a project is ensuring everyone's contributions and feedback are incorporated into the project. By including everyone's expertise, you will ensure that your presentations have the most impact and that no detail was left out. But gathering all of that input and feedback leads to flooded email inboxes, redundant work, and missed communication. You need a way to gather all contributions and all feedback and ensure that it all finds its way into the final presentation.

PowerPoint 2010 provides you with a variety of ways to track, manage, and incorporate contributions from multiple authors into your presentations. Becoming familiar with this functionality will save you countless hours of pouring over multiple versions of the same presentation, and give you the peace of mind that you haven't missed a single edit, comment, or change.

Sections

Sections (2 Slides)

Ask the students what other benefits there may be to dividing a presentation into sections. One possible answer is that it makes it easier to work on large presentations. Encourage remote students to respond in the chat feature or on the white board if it's available.

Sections are organized groups of slides within a presentation that can be added, named, and removed. You can also expand or collapse sections of slides to more easily work with and edit slides in a large presentation. Organizing slides into sections is a good way to split up presentations that will be worked on by several co-authors.

 Access the Checklist tile on your LogicalCHOICE course screen for reference information and job aids on How to Add and Manage Sections

ACTIVITY 5-1
Adding and Managing Sections

Data File

C:\091032Data\Collaborating on a Presentation\Develetech New Products Internal Release_with media.pptx

Scenario

You would like several of Develetech's department heads to review your presentation before you release it to the entire company. But you require their input on only a few of the slides. You decide to divide the presentation using sections, and to collapse the slides the department heads don't need to review for convenience as you edit.

1. Launch the C:\091032Data\Collaborating on a Presentation\Develetech New Products Internal Release_with media.pptx file.

2. Add a section to the presentation.
   a) Navigate to slide 6.
   b) Select Home→Slides→Section, and then select **Add Section** from the drop-down menu.

3. Name the newly added section.
   a) Ensure the new **Untitled Section** is selected in the left pane.
   b) In the **Slides** group, select **Section**.
   c) Select **Rename Section** from the drop-down menu.
   d) In the **Rename Section** dialog box, type *Slides for Review* in the **Section name** field, and then select **Rename**.

4. Move a slide into the **Slides for Review** section.
   a) Select View→Presentation Views→Slide Sorter.
   b) Drag slide 5 from the **Default Section** into the **Slides for Review** section so that it is the first slide in the **Slides for Review** section.
   c) Select **Normal** in the **Presentation Views** group.

5. Collapse the **Default Section** by selecting the **Collapse Section** button on the **Default Section** title.

6. Save the presentation as *My_Develetech New Products Internal Release_with media.pptx*.

Comments

Comments are messages that reviewers can insert into the slides in a presentation without disturbing the slide content. You can attach a comment to a letter, a word, or the entire slide. Comments are often used to provide feedback upon reviewing a presentation or to direct others who are collaborating on the same project. You don't have to delete such comments to prevent them from printing. Comments do not appear on slides during a slide show, do not print, and their spelling cannot be checked. You can access the commands for adding and managing comments in the **Comments** section of the **Review** tab.

Comments

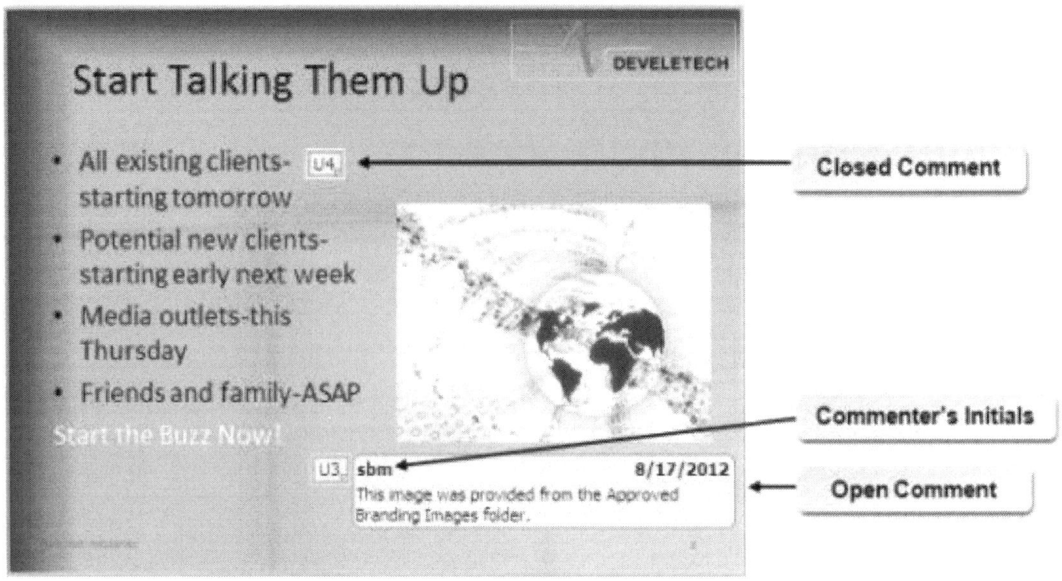

Figure 5-1: Comments displayed on a slide in a presentation.

Markup

Markup refers to any visible changes or edits made to the content, specifically the text, in a document. In PowerPoint 2010, "Markup" refers to comments and also to ink annotations that you can draw on slides by using **Pointer Options** during a slide show.

Tell the students you'll cover **Pointer Options** in the next lesson.

	Access the Checklist tile on your LogicalCHOICE course screen for reference information and job aids on How to Add and Manage Comments

ACTIVITY 5-2
Adding and Managing Comments

Scenario

One of the department heads you asked to review the presentation sent the file back to you in an email message, seeking clarification on where you obtained some of the information. She wants to check with some of the sources herself before approving the content in your presentation. You decide to add comments to the slides to respond to her questions.

---

1. Add a comment to the slide.
   a) If necessary, navigate to slide 5.
   b) Select **Review→Comments→New Comment**.
   c) Type *These descriptions came from last fall's marketing committee forum.*
   d) Click outside the comment to close it.

2. Add a comment to specific text.
   a) Navigate to slide 7.
   b) Select the text in the third bullet point.
   c) Select **New Comment**, and then type *IT has confirmed all new information will be updated to the Wiki daily.*
   d) Click outside the comment.

3. Add a comment to a graphic.
   a) Navigate to slide 8, and then select the image of the globe.
   b) Select **New Comment**, and then type *This image was provided from the Approved Branding Images list.*
   c) Close the comment.

4. Review your comments.
   a) Navigate to slide 5, and then select the closed comment to review it.
   b) Click outside the comment, and then select **Next** in the **Comments** group.
   c) If necessary, select the closed comment to review it.
   d) Select **Next** to review the final comment.

5. Edit the comment.
   a) If necessary, select the closed comment to display its content.
   b) Select **Edit Comment**, and then select the word "list" at the end of the sentence.
   c) Type the word *folder* to replace the existing text, and then click outside the comment to close it.

6. Save the presentation.

Co-authoring

Co-authoring refers to the process by which multiple authors can simultaneously change a single presentation that is stored on a server. Co-authoring a presentation in PowerPoint requires either SharePoint Foundation 2010 or a Windows Live SkyDrive account. The presentation file is stored on a server, which keeps a record of all edits made by the authors. All authors are able to see who is editing the presentation and where those changes take place. Changes from the various authors can be merged to incorporate changes from all authors.

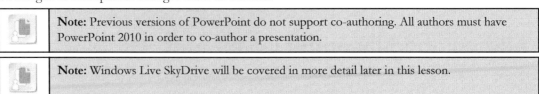

Note: Previous versions of PowerPoint do not support co-authoring. All authors must have PowerPoint 2010 in order to co-author a presentation.

Note: Windows Live SkyDrive will be covered in more detail later in this lesson.

The Revisions Pane

The Revisions Pane

You can also collaborate with other authors on presentations that are not stored on a shared server. The *Revisions pane* lets you compare two versions of a presentation, and then merge particular elements of the two. You can decide to accept or reject any differences between the presentation you have open and the one you are comparing it with. To access the **Revisions** pane, select **Review→Compare→Compare**.

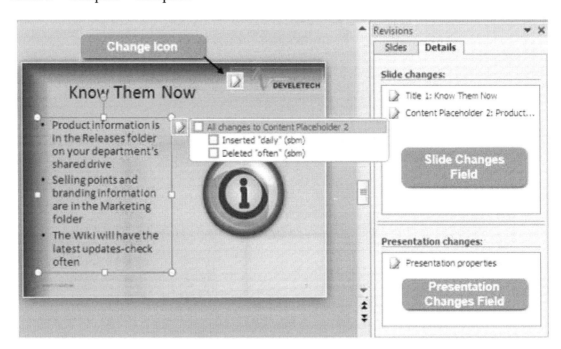

Figure 5–2: The Revisions pane allows you to merge differences between presentations.

Revisions Pane Element	Displays
Change icon	Where changes have been made to the original presentation.
Slides tab	Thumbnail images of any slides in a presentation with changes.
Details tab	Displays the **Slide changes** and the **Presentation changes** fields.
Slide changes field	The element of the slide to which changes have been made.
Presentation changes field	Any changes to the structure of the presentation, such as adding or removing slides.

The Compare Group

The Compare Group

The **Compare** group contains the commands you will use to compare and combine elements within presentations. You can access the **Compare** group from the **Review** tab.

Compare Group Command	Allows You To
Compare	Select a presentation to compare with the one you have open.
Accept	Accept individual changes, all changes on a particular slide, or all changes in a presentation.
Reject	Reject individual changes, all changes on a particular slide, or all changes in a presentation.
Previous	Navigate to the previous change.
Next	Navigate to the next change.
Reviewing Pane	Toggle between displaying and hiding the **Revisions** pane.
End Review	End the presentation comparison, and save the accepted and rejected changes.

 Access the Checklist tile on your LogicalCHOICE course screen for reference information and job aids on How to Compare and Merge Presentations

ACTIVITY 5-3
Comparing and Merging Presentations

Data File

C:\091032Data\Collaborating on a Presentation\Develetech New Products Internal Release_revised.pptx

Scenario

You have received a revised version of your presentation from one of Develetech's department heads. You need to compare the revisions with your original file to determine which changes you would like to keep. You decide to use the Compare and Merge feature in PowerPoint 2010 to more easily compare the versions of the presentation.

1. Compare the two presentations.
   a) From the **Review** tab, select **Compare→Compare**.
   b) In the **Choose File to Merge with Current Presentation** dialog box, navigate to the C:\091032Data \Collaborating on a Presentation\Develetech New Products Internal Release_revised.pptx file and select **Merge**.
   c) In the **Revisions** pane, ensure that the **Details** tab is selected.

2. Accept the first change.
   a) If necessary, select the change icon on the slide to view the change.
   b) In the **Compare** group, select the **Accept down arrow**, and then select **Accept Change**.

3. Accept the next change.
   a) In the **Compare** group, select **Next**.
   b) In the **check boxes** pane next to the change icon, check the **All changes to Title 1** check box.
   c) To toggle between the original text and the revised text, uncheck and check the **All changes to Title 1** check box.
   d) Ensure that the **All changes to Title 1** check box is checked, and then select **Next** in the **Compare** group.

4. Reject the next change.
   a) In the **Slide changes** section of the **Revisions** pane, select **Title 1: Know Them Now**.
   b) Check the **Inserted "Get to" (User)** check box next to the change icon.
   c) In the **Compare** group, select the **Reject down arrow**, and then select **Reject change**.

5. Accept the next change.
   a) In the **Slide changes** section of the **Revisions** pane, select **Content Placeholder 2**.
   b) In the **Compare** group, select **Accept**, and then select **Next**.

6. Accept the final change by selecting **Accept**.

7. End the review and save your changes.
   a) In the **Compare** group, select **End Review**.
   b) In the **Microsoft PowerPoint** dialog box, select **Yes**.

8. Save the presentation to the C:\091032Data\Collaborating on a Presentation folder as *My_Develetech New Products Internal Release_revised.pptx*.

TOPIC B

Publish Slides to a Slide Library

In organizations, especially in large ones, it is not uncommon for slides to appear in multiple presentations for various purposes. Big projects and company-wide initiatives typically revolve around a core concept or idea that applies to all departments within an organization. To maintain a consistent message across various departments, people often reuse images, title slides, charts, tables, and other content to maintain the core vision driving a big project. Sharing these slides via email or a common network drive can lead to an increase in network traffic, outdated versions of slides, and missing content.

PowerPoint 2010, along with other Microsoft services, gives you the ability to publish commonly used slides in a central location where they can be updated, secured, and versioned. By taking advantage of these capabilities, you can greatly increase efficiency across entire organizations, while keeping everybody up to date with the latest changes to shared content.

Slide Libraries

Slide Libraries

This is a good opportunity to poll the class. What types of slides do they think should not be published to a slide library? Possible answers: anything with confidential information, slides not likely to be used often. Check in for responses from remote students.

A *slide library* is a server-based repository for PowerPoint slides. Slide libraries allow multiple users to share and reuse slides. Slides published to a slide library upload as individual files. This makes it easy to update and track changes made to the slides in a library. When you reuse a slide from a slide library, the slide library maintains a link to your presentation. When changes are made to the slides in the library, you will receive a notification, and have the option to accept or reject the changes, or replace the slide with another. In order to create and use slide libraries, you must have access to a Microsoft SharePoint server running SharePoint Foundation 2010.

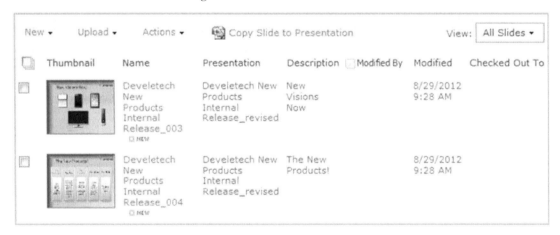

Figure 5-3: Slides published to a slide library.

Microsoft SharePoint 2010

Microsoft SharePoint 2010 is a server-based service that provides a central repository for files. Files on a SharePoint server can be accessed, modified, and saved from various locations. SharePoint allows users to control access to, share, collaborate on, and keep track of a variety of files. SharePoint can also track information about users who access files and the date and time of the activity, and can facilitate file versioning.

The Publish Slides Dialog Box

You can publish slides you wish to save in a slide library by using the **Publish Slides** dialog box. From here you can select which slides you wish to save, and the library to which to publish them in. You can access the **Publish Slides** dialog box by selecting **File→Save & Send→Publish Slides**, and then selecting the **Publish Slides** button in the right pane.

The Publish Slides
Dialog Box

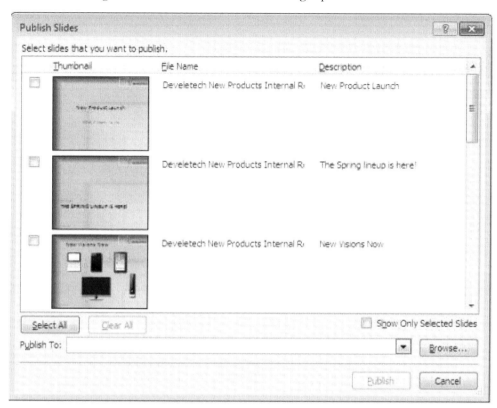

Figure 5-4: Slides in the Publish Slides dialog box.

 Note: To publish slides to a slide library, you must be using PowerPoint Professional Plus 2010.

Access the Checklist tile on your LogicalCHOICE course screen for reference information and job aids on How to Publish and Reuse Slides

ACTIVITY 5-4
Publishing and Reusing Slides (Optional)

Data File

C:\091032Data\Collaborating on a Presentation\Develetech comms template.potx

Before You Begin

Microsoft Office PowerPoint 2010 Professional Plus is installed, and you have access to an existing SharePoint Slide Library.

You have a Windows Live ID account.

> **Note:** If you are using a Windows Live ID that you created or that your instructor created for you solely for the purposes of this course, you may wish to delete the account when you are finished taking the course. To deactivate a Windows Live ID account, go to https://login.live.com/, log in using your credentials, select **Close account** from the bottom of the **Account summary** page, and follow the prompts.

Scenario

While reviewing your presentation, several people suggested that some of your slides would be useful in a number of other presentations. Develetech has a SharePoint library set up for publishing PowerPoint slides. You decide to publish the reusable slides to the slide library for others to use, and to verify that the slides have been published successfully.

---

1. Publish slides 3 and 5 to a slide library.
   a) Select **File→Save & Send→Publish Slides**, and then select **Publish Slides** from the right pane.
   b) In the **Publish Slides** dialog box, check the check boxes for slides 3 and 5.
   c) Select **Browse**, navigate to the desired slide library, and then select **Select**, or, in the **Publish to** field, enter the URL for the desired slide library.
   d) Select **Publish**.
   e) If prompted, enter your login credentials.
   f) Save the presentation and leave the file open.

Provide the students with the target URL if the slide library has not already been opened and saved in My Slide Libraries on the local system.

2. Verify that the slides are available in the slide library.
   a) Open the C:\091032Data\Collaborating on a Presentation\Develetech comms template.potx file.
   b) Navigate to the **C:\091032Data\Collaborating on a Presentation** folder and save the file as *My_Develetech comms template.pptx*.
   c) Select **Home→New Slide down arrow→Reuse Slides**.
   d) In the **Reuse Slides** pane, in the **Insert slide from** field, enter the URL for the desired slide library. Or, select **Browse→Browse Slide Library**, navigate to the desired slide library, and then select **Select**.
   e) If you entered the URL, select the arrow button 🔘.
   f) If prompted, enter your login credentials.
   g) Select and insert the slides you added to the slide library in step 1.
   h) Close the **Reuse Slides** pane.
   i) Save and close the file. Leave **My_Develetech New Products Internal Release_revised.pptx** open.

TOPIC C

Share a Presentation on the Web

There may be cases in which a people collaborating on a presentation do not have PowerPoint available to them. Or, they may need to work on the presentation from multiple devices, such as a desktop computer, a laptop, and a tablet. As people begin to work on presentations on a greater number of devices, and from a greater number of locations, it becomes more important to have a single, central location for accessing your presentation files.

PowerPoint 2010 gives you the ability to share your presentation with collaborators on the web. This means anyone on your team can access a single, up-to-date version of the project file from a variety of devices, whether or not PowerPoint is installed on the device, and from nearly any location. Sharing your presentations on the web will help ensure that everyone's contributions are included, that no one is performing unnecessary work, and that nothing gets lost in the mix.

Windows Live SkyDrive

Windows Live SkyDrive is a server-based file storage service that allows you to upload, share, and set permissions for various file types. By default, SkyDrive provides you with a **Documents** folder and a **Pictures** folder for storing files you do not wish to share. There is also a **Public** folder in which you can share files you wish to share with others. You can also create new folders and set permissions for various people. You can allow others to edit the files you share with them, or give them read-only access.

Windows Live SkyDrive

This is a good opportunity to poll students about security concerns they may have. What are some of the dangers they see with sharing content online?

> **Note:** In order to edit a shared presentation, the recipient will need to sign in using his or her Windows Live ID/Windows SkyDrive credentials. However, the recipient can view the presentation without logging in.

The Save to Web Option

The *Save to Web option* allows you to save your presentations online by using your Windows Live ID. When you access the Save to Web option from PowerPoint 2010, you are prompted to sign in to your Windows Live account. Once you have signed in, you can save your presentations to your Windows Live SkyDrive folders. The Save to Web option allows you to access and share your presentations on the web, where you or others can review and, to some degree, edit the presentations.

The Save to Web Option

The PowerPoint Web App

The *PowerPoint web application (or Web App)* lets you access, view, and edit the presentations you save to SkyDrive online. With the PowerPoint Web App, you have two options for working with a presentation: You can view and edit the presentation directly from your web browser, or you can download the presentation and work with it in PowerPoint 2010. When you select the **Edit in Browser** feature, there are some limitations to the PowerPoint functionality, and all edits are automatically saved.

The PowerPoint Web App

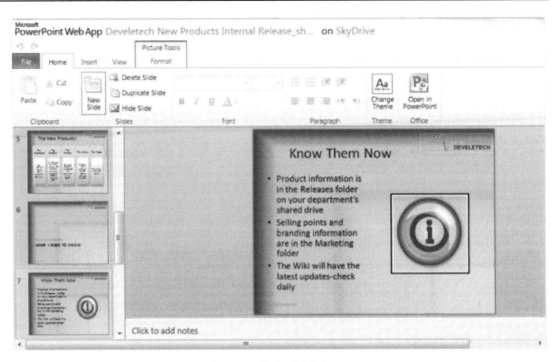

Figure 5-5: A presentation open in the PowerPoint Web App.

Note: To further explore the PowerPoint Web App, you can access the LearnTO **Edit Presentations with the PowerPoint Web App** presentation from the **LearnTO** tile on the LogicalCHOICE Course screen.

Access the Checklist tile on your LogicalCHOICE course screen for reference information and job aids on How to Share a Presentation on the Web

You may want to show LearnTO **Edit Presentations with the PowerPoint Web App** from the LogicalCHOICE Course screen or have students navigate out to the Course screen and watch it themselves as a supplement to your instruction. If not, please remind students to visit the LearnTOs for this course on their LogicalCHOICE Course screen after class for supplemental information and additional resources.

ACTIVITY 5-5
Sharing a Presentation on the Web

Before You Begin

Pair up with a partner for the activity. One of you will play the role of the communications director; the other will play the role of the VP of marketing and branding.

You have a Windows Live ID and a Windows Live SkyDrive account.

> **Note:** Make sure you have access to your login credentials for your Microsoft accounts.

> **Note:** If you are using a Windows Live ID that you created or that your instructor created for you solely for the purposes of this course, you may wish to delete the account when you are finished taking the course. To deactivate a Windows account, go to https://login.live.com/, log in using your credentials, select **Close account** from the bottom of the **Account summary** page, and follow the prompts.

Scenario

You (the communications director) need final approval from the VP of marketing and branding before you can distribute your New Product Launch presentation to all Develetech employees. However, the VP is traveling outside the country and will not always have access to her laptop. You decide to share the presentation with the VP on the web, allowing her to make edits to the presentation whether she has her own computer or not.

You can participate if you have an odd number of students. If time permits, students can perform the activity twice, switching roles for each turn.

Remote students are encouraged to use the private chat feature in their web conferencing tool to communicate with their partners to avoid congestion on the audio feed.

Encourage one of the students playing the role of the communications director to share his or her screen while performing the activity. This will give the students who are waiting to participate the opportunity to view the procedure.

Remember that Microsoft may make changes to the online environment at any time.

1. Communications director: Save the presentation to the web.
   a) Select **File→Save & Send→Save to Web** and, from the **Save to Windows Live** pane, select **Sign In**.
   b) In the **Connecting to docs.live.net** dialog box, enter your Windows Live ID email address and password in the associated fields and select **OK**.
   c) In the **Microsoft SkyDrive** section of the **Save to Microsoft SkyDrive** pane, select the **Public** folder in the **Shared Folders** section, and then select **Save As**.

> **Note:** It takes a few moments for the **Save As** dialog box to launch.

   d) In the **Save As** dialog box, type *Develetech New Products Release_shared file* in the **File name** field, and then select **Save**.

> **Note:** Make sure the file has completely uploaded to SkyDrive before closing the presentation. While the upload is still occurring, a progress bar is displayed on the status bar.

   e) Close the presentation.

2. Communications director: Share the presentation with VP of marketing and branding.
   a) Launch your web browser, navigate to https://skydrive.live.com/, enter your login credentials, and select **Sign in**.
   b) Ensure the files and folders are displaying in **List** view by selecting the **List** button near the top-right of the screen ☰ .
   c) In the **Files** pane, select the **Public** folder.

d) Check the check box next to the **Develetech New Products Release_shared file.pptx** file, and then select **Sharing** from the command bar along the top of the screen.

e) Enter the email address for the VP of marketing and branding in the **To** field.

> **Note:** Make sure you enter the email address associated with your partner's Windows Live ID/Windows SkyDrive account. In order use the PowerPoint Web App to edit presentations, the recipient must log in with a Microsoft account.

f) Ensure the **Recipients can edit** check box is checked.

g) Select **Share**.

h) If prompted, click the **Please Complete this Security Check** link and follow the instructions.

i) Click **Close** to close the permissions window.

3. VP of marketing and branding: Access and edit the shared presentation.

a) Launch your web browser, navigate to and log in to your email account, and view the email from your partner.

b) Click the **Develetech New Products Release_shared file.pptx** link.

c) If necessary, select **Unblock** and close any other warnings.

d) View the presentation in your web browser by using the navigation controls at the bottom of the screen.

e) Select **EDIT PRESENTATION→Edit in PowerPoint** from the menu bar near the top of the screen.

f) If prompted, select **Continue** to verify your account.

g) In the **Open Document** dialog box, select **OK**.

h) Enter your Windows Live ID/Windows SkyDrive credentials in the appropriate fields and select **OK**.

i) Navigate to slide 7.

j) Select **Enable Editing**.

k) In the second bullet point, change the first word from "Selling" to "Talking."

l) Select **File→Save**, and then close the presentation.

m) Close your web browser.

4. Communications director: Launch the presentation to view the change.

a) If necessary, navigate to and log in to your SkyDrive account.

b) If necessary, select the **Public** folder.

c) Check the **Develetech New Products Release_shared file.pptx** check box, select the **Open down arrow** from the menu bar, and then select **Open in PowerPoint**.

d) In the **Open Document** dialog box, select **OK**.

e) If prompted, in the **Connecting to d.docs.live.net** dialog box, enter your Windows Live ID/Windows SkyDrive credentials, and then select **OK**.

f) Navigate to slide 7, and then verify the change has been made.

If the changes don't appear, close PowerPoint and the browser and try again in a few seconds.

5. Time permitting, repeat the activity, switching roles. The new communications director will have to re-open C:\091032Data\Collaborating on a Presentation\My_Develetech New Products Internal Release_revised.pptx.

> **Note:** It is recommended that both participants close their browsers before switching roles and repeating the activity.

6. Close all open presentations.

Summary

In this lesson, you collaborated on a presentation to leverage the skills, knowledge, and experience of everyone on your team. Your presentation contains a variety of engaging, informative content, and has been reviewed, edited, and polished by everyone whose expertise was required to craft your message.

Can you think of additional uses for comments in a presentation other than for giving feedback?

A: Answers will vary, but could include leaving development notes for yourself because comments don't display during a slide show.

Do you think the ability to store and access your work online will significantly change the way you perform your job?

A: Answers will vary, with some students being likely to jump at the chance to have a single, convenient point of access for storing, sharing, and accessing work. Concerns about reliability and security, however, may keep some people from relying too heavily on cloud-based services.

Have any of the students experienced losing files or a breach of security while using a cloud-based service? Remember to check in with remote students as well.

 Note: Check your LogicalCHOICE Course screen for opportunities to interact with your classmates, peers, and the larger LogicalCHOICE online community about the topics covered in this course or other topics you are interested in. From the Course screen you can also access available resources for a more continuous learning experience.

Encourage students to use the social networking tools provided on the LogicalCHOICE Home screen to follow up with their peers after the course is completed for further discussion and resources to support continued learning.

6 Customizing a Slide Show

Lesson Time: 1 hour

Lesson Objectives

In this lesson, you will customize a slide show. You will:

- Annotate a presentation

- Set up a slide show

- Create a custom slide show

- Add hyperlinks and action buttons

- Record a presentation

Lesson Introduction

Most organizations are made up of departments or groups that combine to create an overall entity. As such, organizations often have a need for information to be delivered to a variety of audiences that all have different needs. You and your team have put a lot of time and effort in to creating a high-impact, well-polished presentation, and you don't want to have to create different versions of the presentation for different audiences. Additionally, you don't want your presentation to be inflexible during an event. Discussions often take different directions when the audience begins to interact with the presenter.

PowerPoint 2010 provides you with the ability to tailor your presentations to the exact needs of your audience. You can use the same presentation even when you have half the time or you can't be there in person for the event. And, you can annotate your existing content without altering the presentation file, so that you have a fresh, clean file every time you present. Understanding how to take advantage of these options means you will be ready to deliver your message regardless of the situation, without a lot of rework.

TOPIC A

Annotate a Presentation

Regardless of how much thought and planning you put into developing your presentation, you simply cannot account for every situation that may arise during the presentation event. Audience members ask questions, conversations sometimes go off on a tangent, and visuals are not always fully understood by the audience. Presentations are, after all, live events that live and breathe. A truly engaging presentation is one in which there is interaction between the audience and the presenter. As such, it is necessary to examine your slides and the content they contain by taking notes, highlighting key points, and identifying concepts that don't work well or content that may be inaccurate.

PowerPoint 2010 gives you the ability to mark up your presentation during the live event. You can take notes on your slides when people bring up important points, highlight text you wish to return to, or point out particular visual elements to clarify your message. Understanding how these interactive tools work will elevate your presentation from a one-way lecture to dialogue that encourages audience participation.

Annotations

Annotations

This is a good opportunity to poll the class or engage in a discussion. Have they experienced a time when the annotation tools would have been useful? Encourage remote learners to respond via the video link if it's available.

Annotations are markings you can place on the slides during a presentation to highlight key points, add emphasis to content, or to identify content you may wish to return to. PowerPoint 2010 gives you the ability to annotate your slides during a presentation.

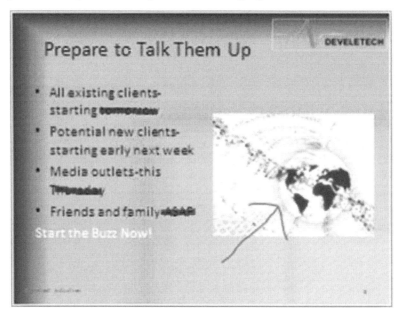

Figure 6-1: Annotations on a PowerPoint slide.

Annotation Tools

You can use the *annotation tools* in PowerPoint 2010 to mark your presentation slides during a slide show. Several annotation tools are available to suit a variety of uses.

Annotation Tool	Is Used To
Arrow	Point to and select on-screen elements during a slide show. This is the default state of the mouse pointer.
Pen	Write on the slide during a slide show.
Highlighter	Highlight important on-screen objects or text.
Ink Color	Change the color of the pen or the highlighter.
Eraser	Erase a single annotation mark.
Erase All Ink on Slide	Erase all on-screen annotations.
Arrow Options	Set the visibility of the pointer.

Access the Checklist tile on your LogicalCHOICE course screen for reference information and job aids on How to Annotate a Presentation

To view the annotation tools available all of the time, add them to a custom group on the ribbon.

ACTIVITY 6-1
Annotating a Presentation

Data File

C:\091032Data\Customizing a Slide Show\Develetech New Products Internal Release_final version.pptx

Scenario

Your presentation has been reviewed by all of Develetech's department heads and several VPs. You have incorporated all feedback and feel the presentation is nearly ready to be distributed. However, you aren't sure whether or not some of the images on your slides adhere to Develetech's visual guidelines. You ask one of the company's graphic designers to review the images with you. Because he works in a separate building, you decide to use web conferencing to review the presentation together. You use PowerPoint's annotation tools to point out specific areas of concern.

 Note: During this activity, if you are using web conferencing software in your class, do not actually share your desktop or the PowerPoint 2010 application.

1. Launch the C:\091032Data\Customizing a Slide Show\Develetech New Products Internal Release_final version.pptx file.

2. Navigate to slide 7 and select **Slide Show→Start Slide Show→From Current Slide**.

3. Use the **Pen** tool to annotate the presentation.
   a) Right-click the screen, select **Pointer Options**, and then select **Pen** from the secondary menu.
   b) Click and hold the left mouse button, and then drag the **Pen** tool to draw a circle around the highlight on the image of the circle.
   c) Advance to the next slide, and then draw a line below Africa on the image of the globe.

4. Use the **Highlighter** to annotate the presentation.
   a) Advance to the next slide, right-click the screen, and select **Pointer Options→Highlighter**.
   b) Right-click the screen and select **Pointer Options→Ink Color**.
   c) Select a color from the tertiary menu.
   d) Click and drag the mouse to highlight the dark blue wedge at the bottom of the pie chart and the bars along the bottom of the image.

5. Press the **Esc** key to deactivate the highlighter, and then exit the slide show.

6. In the **Microsoft PowerPoint** dialog box, select **Discard** to delete all annotations.

TOPIC B

Set Up a Slide Show

You may be called upon to deliver your presentation in a number of different environments. Although the most common type of presentation is delivered live in front of an audience, you may need to set one up to be viewed by members of the public on a display in a high-traffic area. Or, you may need to email the presentation to be viewed by individuals using computers or tablets. Delivering your presentation in these various manners will, naturally, require different methods of running the presentation.

PowerPoint 2010 provides you with the ability to run your presentations remotely, take complete control of your presentation in a live environment without distracting the audience, and control how individuals can view your presentations on their own computers. Understanding how to set up and run these various presentation types provides you with the capability and flexibility to deliver your message to a wider audience without having to schedule, attend, and present at numerous live events.

The Presenter View

Presenter view allows you to display different views of your presentation for yourself and for the audience. This feature allows you to view notes pages or preview upcoming slides while the audience views the presentation as a slide show from a projector or separate monitor. To take advantage of the feature, your computer must have multiple display capabilities.

The Presenter View

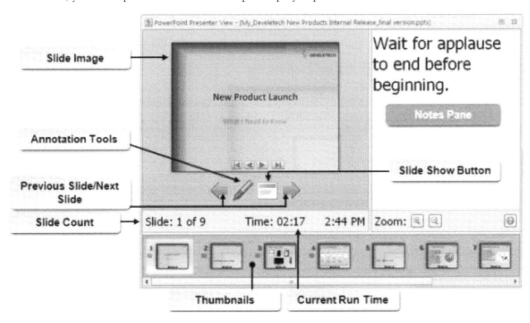

Figure 6–2: The Presenter view lets you control the presentation without disrupting the audience's view.

Presenter View Element	Function
Slide Image	Displays the slide currently being viewed by the audience.
Notes Pane	Displays speaker notes to the presenter.
Previous Slide Button	Navigates to the previous slide or animation.

Presenter View Element	Function
Pointer Options Button	Provides access to the annotation tools.
Slide Show Button	Provides access to navigation commands.
Next Slide Button	Navigates to the next slide or animation.
Slide Count	Displays the current slide number and the total number of slides in the presentation.
Current Presentation Run Time	Displays the current elapsed time of the presentation. This feature is active whether you are using manual navigation or timed slides.
Clock	Displays the current time.
Zoom In/Out Buttons	Allows you to set the zoom level for the speaker notes text.
Thumbnails	Display thumbnail previews or the slides in the presentation.

Kiosks

Kiosks are displays that are set up in public or high-traffic locations, such as trade shows, malls, or lobbies. Kiosks often contain computer or video monitors that display information to the public. You can set up PowerPoint presentations to display at kiosks and customize how much control viewers have over running the slide show.

Looping

In PowerPoint *looping* refers to the process of automatically playing a presentation repeatedly. A looped presentation will automatically replay from the first slide once the final slide is displayed.

The Set Up Show Dialog Box

The Set Up Show Dialog Box

The **Set Up Show** dialog box gives you access to the commands you will use to set up your slide shows. The **Set Up Show** dialog box is divided into various sections that contain related commands. You can access the **Set Up Show** dialog box in the **Set Up** group on the **Slide Show** tab.

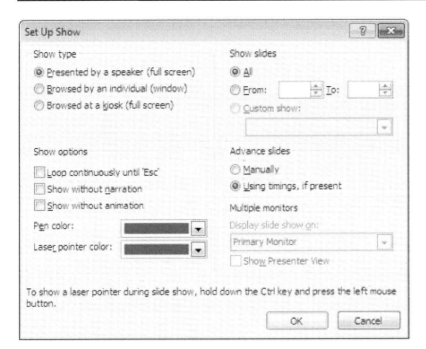

Figure 6-3: The Set Up Show dialog box.

The **Set Up Show** dialog box is divided into five sections.

Set Up Show Dialog Box Section	Provides Commands For
Show type	Choosing presentations that will be presented by a speaker, viewed by an individual, or displayed at a kiosk. The right-click menu options are different for a speaker than for an individual, and the individual's slide show plays in a window that can be restored or minimized (instead of full screen). In a kiosk presentation, there are no right-click options.
Show slides	Selecting which slides will be displayed during a presentation.
Show options	Looping a presentation, and displaying a presentation with or without narration and animation.
Advance slides	Determining how the presentation will advance during a slide show.
Multiple monitors	Determining which monitor a slide show will display on.

 Access the Checklist tile on your LogicalCHOICE course screen for reference information and job aids on How to Set Up a Slide Show

ACTIVITY 6-2
Setting Up a Slide Show

Scenario

The graphic designer informed you that all of the images in your presentation comply with Develetech's visual guidelines, so your presentation is final. Since most of the people who will view the presentation will do so at their computers, you decide to set the presentation to be viewed by an individual.

1. In the **Set Up** group, select **Set Up Slide Show**.

2. Set the presentation to be viewed by an individual.
   a) In the **Set Up Show** dialog box, in the **Show type** section, select the **Browsed by an individual (window)** radio button.
   b) If necessary, in the **Advance slides** section, select the **Using timings, if present** radio button.
   c) Select **OK**.

3. Save the file to the C:\091032Data\Customizing a Slide Show folder as *My_Develetech New Products Internal Release_final version.pptx*.

TOPIC C

Create a Custom Slide Show

You may not always need to display your entire presentation to all audiences. Certain segments of your presentation may be relevant to some audiences, but not to others. Or you may be allotted different amounts of time when presenting at various events. Rather than creating a separate presentation for the various situations, you will likely wish to select which slides in your existing presentation you will need to display to the various audiences.

PowerPoint 2010 allows you to create custom slide shows to present only those slides relevant to particular audiences. Creating custom slide shows will allow you to leverage the presentation you have already created, while giving you the flexibility to adapt it to a variety of situations and timelines.

Custom Slide Shows

Custom slide shows are presentations that display only a selected sequence of slides. Setting up custom slide shows does not alter the content of the existing slide show, nor the original sequence of slides. Custom slide shows only affect which slides are displayed and in which order.

The Custom Shows Dialog Box

The **Custom Shows** dialog box allows you to manage the custom slide shows you have created for a particular presentation. From the **Custom Shows** dialog box, you can create, edit, and delete the custom slide shows associated with the presentation. You can access the **Custom Shows** dialog box from the **Custom Slide Show** drop-down menu in the **Start Slide Show** group on the **Slide Show** tab.

The Custom Shows Dialog Box

Figure 6-4: The Custom Shows dialog box.

The Define Custom Show Dialog Box

The **Define Custom Show** dialog box allows you name, add slides to, and reorder slides in a custom slide show. You can access the **Define Custom Show** dialog box by selecting **New** in the **Custom Shows** dialog box.

The Define Custom Show Dialog Box

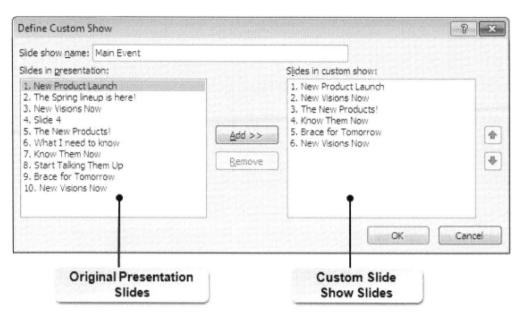

Figure 6-5: The Define Custom Show dialog box.

 Access the Checklist tile on your LogicalCHOICE course screen for reference information and job aids on How to Create a Custom Slide Show

ACTIVITY 6-3
Creating a Custom Slide Show

Scenario

The VP of sales asked you to provide some key sales reps with a version of the presentation to show to big Develetech distributors. He doesn't think the target audience needs to view all of the slides, so he asked you to remove some of them. You feel you should also rearrange some of the other slides so the presentation makes sense given the changes. Instead of creating a whole separate file, you decide to set up a custom slide show for the sales reps to use when presenting the new products.

1. In the **Start Slide Show** group, select **Custom Slide Show→Custom Shows**.

2. In the **Custom Shows** dialog box, select **New**.

3. In the **Define Custom Show** dialog box, in the **Slide show name** field, type *Sales Reps Custom Show*.

4. In the **Slides in presentation** field, select slides 1, 2, 3, 5, 7, 8, and 10, and then select **Add**.

    Note: You can select multiple slides to move at once by pressing and holding down the **Ctrl** key while selecting the slides.

5. In the **Slides in custom show** field, select slide 4, and then select the **up arrow button** to move it up in the order.

6. Select **OK**, verify the new custom slide show is displayed in the **Custom shows** field, and then select **Show** to review the custom slide show.

7. Exit the slide show and save the file.

TOPIC D

Add Hyperlinks and Action Buttons

Although you can include content from a variety of sources within a presentation, you may also wish to display items that cannot be directly inserted into PowerPoint. For example, if you are leading a training presentation for a particular software application, it may be necessary to launch the application to demonstrate a particular procedure. Or, there may be supplemental information on various web sites that you wish to display during any number of presentations. You cannot place a web page or an application within a presentation.

PowerPoint 2010 does, however, allow to you link to external resources or launch applications from objects within your presentation. By inserting these links or actions into your presentations, you will be able to take advantage of a limitless number of resources, and increase the effectiveness and the appeal of your presentations.

Hyperlinks

Hyperlinks

Hyperlinks are navigational commands within documents or on web pages used to jump to other documents, other web pages, or another location within the current document. Hyperlinks can be created by using either text or images. Typically, but not always, text containing a hyperlink is displayed as blue text that is underlined. You can add hyperlinks to any slide in your PowerPoint presentations. In addition to textual hyperlinks, in PowerPoint, you can create hyperlinks from images, shapes, graphs, and WordArt.

The Insert Hyperlink Dialog Box

The Insert Hyperlink Dialog Box

The **Insert Hyperlink** dialog box allows you to create hyperlinks from text and objects in your presentation. You can access the **Insert Hyperlink** dialog box from the **Links** group on the **Insert** tab.

Figure 6-6: The Existing File or Web Page option on the Insert Hyperlink dialog box.

The available commands in the **Insert Hyperlink** dialog box will vary depending on which **Link to** option is selected. However, the following commands always appear.

Insert Hyperlink Dialog Box Command	Function
Link To Options	Determine the target for the hyperlink. Selecting from among these options will affect which commands/options are available in the dialog box.
Text To Display field	Displays the text that has been selected to create the hyperlink. This field is grayed out when an object is selected for the hyperlink.
Screen Tip button	Is used to create a screen tip that appears when the mouse pointer is hovered over the hyperlink.

Action Buttons

Action buttons are on-screen objects used to perform pre-determined functions. You can use action buttons to navigate to other slides or presentations, launch a program, run a macro, or play an audio file. Action buttons can be triggered by selecting them or by hovering the mouse pointer over them.

Action Buttons

 Note: Creating and editing macros requires the use of Visual Basic for Applications and will not be covered in this course. You can find more information on creating and editing macros at Office.com.

 Note: To further explore action buttons, you can access the LearnTO **Effectively Use Action Buttons in Your Presentations** presentation from the **LearnTO** tile on the LogicalCHOICE Course screen.

The Action Settings Dialog Box

The **Action Settings** dialog box contains the commands you will use to configure action settings in your presentations. It is split into two tabs: the **Mouse Click** tab and the **Mouse Over** tab. You can access the **Action Settings** dialog box from the **Links** group on the **Insert** tab.

You may want to show LearnTO **Effectively Use Action Buttons in Your Presentations** from the LogicalCHOICE Course screen or have students navigate out to the Course screen and watch it themselves as a supplement to your instruction. If not, please remind students to visit the LearnTOs for this course on their LogicalCHOICE Course screen after class for supplemental information and additional resources.

Action Settings Dialog Box Command	Function
None radio button	Assigns no action button functionality to the object.
Hyperlink To radio button	Assigns a hyperlink to the object.
Run Program radio button	Sets the object as a trigger to run a specified program.
Run Macro radio button	Sets the object as a trigger to run a specified macro.
Object Action radio button	Sets a linked or embedded object as a trigger to perform an action.
Play Sound check box	Assigns a sound effect to the object.
Highlight Click/Highlight When Mouse Over check box	Sets the object to be highlighted whenever clicked or hovered over with the mouse pointer.

The Action Settings Dialog Box

 Access the Checklist tile on your LogicalCHOICE course screen for reference information and job aids on How to Add Hyperlinks and Action Buttons

ACTIVITY 6-4
Adding Action Buttons to a Presentation

Scenario

Some of your slides are timed, but not all of them. The audience will have to navigate through some of the slides on their own. You decide it would be a good idea to add action buttons to help the audience more easily navigate the presentation. As you want the action buttons on all of the slides, you decide to add them to the slide master.

1. Select the slide master.
   a) Select View→Master Views→Slide Master.
   b) Select the **slide master** in the left pane.

   > **Note:** Remember the slide master is the large thumbnail at the top of the left pane in the **Slide Master** view. Make sure you select the **slide master** and not a **slide layout**.

2. Add an action button.
   a) Select Insert→Illustrations→Shapes.
   b) In the **Shapes** gallery, in the **Action Buttons** section, select **Action Button: Beginning** ◁ .
   c) Draw the action button near the **footer placeholder** at the bottom left of the slide so that it is approximately the same height as the **footer placeholder**, leaving room for three additional action buttons between the **footer** and the **page number placeholders**.
   d) In the **Action Settings** dialog box, from the **Mouse Click** tab, ensure that the **Hyperlink to** radio button is selected and that **First Slide** is selected in the **Hyperlink to** field.
   e) Add a sound to play when clicked by checking the **Play sound** check box, and then selecting the desired sound effect from the **Play sound** drop-down menu.
   f) Select OK.

3. Repeat step 2 three more times, adding the following action buttons to form a row, in order, from left to right, between the footer placeholder and the page number placeholder: **Action Button: Back or Previous** ◁ , **Action Button: Forward or Next** ▷ , and **Action Button: End** ▷| .

   > **Note:** The default settings are a bit different depending on the action button you are adding. Ensure the settings in the **Hyperlink to** field in the **Action Settings** dialog box are appropriate for each of the action buttons.

Check in with students frequently during this activity. Encourage remote students to share their desktops so that you can monitor their progress.

4. Resize and arrange the action buttons so that they are centered between the footer placeholder and the page number placeholder, and so that they are the same size and shape.

5. Apply shape styles to the action buttons.
   a) Group the action buttons together by selecting all of the buttons, selecting **Drawing Tools contextual tab→Arrange→Group**, and then selecting **Group** from the drop-down menu.
   b) In the **Shape Styles** group, select the **More** button on the **Shape Styles** gallery.
   c) Select the desired style.

6. Select Slide Master→Close→Close Master View.

7. Verify that the action buttons display on all of the slides in the presentation, and that they perform the appropriate action during the slide show.

8. Save the presentation.

TOPIC E

Record a Presentation

It is often the case that not all people who need to be present for an event are able to attend. And there is often a need for certain presentations to be delivered numerous times when the speaker isn't necessarily available. You may find that you need to record a version of your presentation to be delivered at different times in different locations. Additionally, you may find yourself in the situation of having to drive the presentation, but you cannot be near the device it's loaded on. Simply put, there are a lot of situations in which recording elements of your presentation is necessary.

PowerPoint 2010 gives you the ability to rehearse your slide timings as you deliver your presentation, allowing you to time the advancement of your slides in sync with your delivery. And, with the addition of a microphone, you can record your narration. These capabilities allow you to create user-independent presentations, meaning you can figuratively be in several places at once.

The Record Slide Show Dialog Box

The Record Slide Show Dialog Box

The **Record Slide Show** dialog box allows you to decide whether to record just the slide timings and animations in your presentation, just narration and the laser pointer, or all of these. To access the **Record Slide Show** dialog box, select **Slide Show→Set Up→Record Slide Show**.

The Recording Shortcut Menu

The Recording Shortcut Menu

The **Recording** shortcut menu provides you with the commands you will use to record narration and timing of your presentations. You can record narration to slides ahead of time, or record a live presentation to be shared later. The **Recording** shortcut menu appears along with the slide show as you record a presentation. When you have finished recording a presentation, the presentation will display in the **Slide Sorter** view, with the slide timings displayed below the slides.

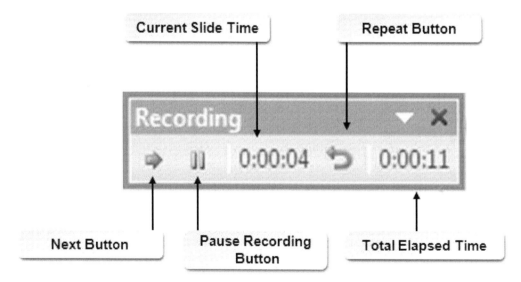

Figure 6-7: Controls on the Recording shortcut menu.

Recording Shortcut Menu Element	Function
Next button	Advances to the next slide, while keeping track of the previous slide's timing.
Pause Recording button	Pauses the recording.
Current Slide Time	Displays the timing of the current slide.
Repeat button	Repeats the current slide from the beginning. This resets the **Current slide time** value, and restores the elapsed time back to where it was when you originally reached the current slide.
Elapsed Time	Displays the total run time of all slides up to the current point in the recording process.

 Note: Your computer must be equipped with a microphone and a sound card in order to record narration.

The Rehearse Timings Feature

The *Rehearse Timings feature* allows you to keep track of your slide timing as you practice delivering your presentation. The rehearse timings feature uses the **Recording** shortcut menu to automatically set your slide timing without recording narration. You can access the **Rehearse Timing** feature by selecting **Slide Show→Set Up→Rehearse Timings**.

 Access the Checklist tile on your LogicalCHOICE course screen for reference information and job aids on How to Record a Presentation

Poll the class. How can the **Rehearse Timings** feature be of benefit if you are not recording narration or slide timings? One possible answer: It can help you rehearse for a presentation that you will drive, to make sure you can meet the time requirements of the event.

ACTIVITY 6-5
Recording a Presentation

Before You Begin
It may be helpful to read this activity in its entirety before beginning.

Scenario
You have timings set for some of the slides in your presentation, but not all of them. You decide you would like the entire presentation to play by itself so viewers don't have to navigate through the slides unless they choose to. You use the Rehearse Timings feature to adjust the slide timing to give viewers a reasonable amount of time to view the content on the slides before they advance automatically.

Ask students to turn down the volume on their computers for this activity. This is especially important if you have remote students. Playing back audio at a high volume can cause feedback in your audio feed. Headphones or earbuds may also be helpful depending on your audio setup.

1. Select **Slide Show→Set Up→Record Slide Show down arrow**, and then select **Start recording from beginning**.

2. Read the text on screen, leaving a reasonable amount of extra time to account for people's differing reading rates, and then select **Next** in the **Recording** shortcut menu.

 Note: To pause the recording at any point during the activity, select **Pause** in the **Recording** shortcut menu. Select **Resume Recording** in the **Microsoft PowerPoint** dialog box to resume recording.

 Note: If at any point in the recording you need to re-time a slide, select **Repeat** in the **Recording** shortcut menu.

3. Repeat step 2 for the second slide.

4. Allow the animations to play out on slide 3 before selecting **Next**.

5. Allow the video to play out on slide 4 before selecting **Next**.

6. Continue this process through the last slide, allow the audio clip to play out, and then select **Close** in the **Recording** shortcut menu.

7. If prompted, in the **Microsoft PowerPoint** dialog box, select **Yes**.

8. View the slide show to verify the slide timings have been applied.

9. Save and close the file.

Summary

In this lesson, you customized a slide show to meet your needs. Your work is nearly complete, and you are ready to deliver your presentation in a wide variety of situations, in front of a number of different audiences.

Would you have any reservations about presenting during a live event by using a fully automated slide show?

A: Answers will vary depending on the person and the specific event. It is likely that most presenters would feel better if they had some form of control by having access to the computer or another person who could drive the slide show if necessary. The amount a person can rehearse is also likely to affect how comfortable he or she would be presenting an automated slide show.

Can you think of a time when creating custom slide shows for various events could have saved you a significant amount of rework?

A: Answers will vary, but students who have had to present at numerous trade shows or other industry-related events have likely been asked to deliver the same presentation in a wide range of timeframes.

Note: Check your LogicalCHOICE Course screen for opportunities to interact with your classmates, peers, and the larger LogicalCHOICE online community about the topics covered in this course or other topics you are interested in. From the Course screen you can also access available resources for a more continuous learning experience.

Check in with remote students. Call on someone you haven't heard from in a while. Remote students can participate via chat or the whiteboard feature on your web conferencing system if it's available.

Encourage students to use the social networking tools provided on the LogicalCHOICE Home screen to follow up with their peers after the course is completed for further discussion and resources to support continued learning.

7 | Securing and Distributing a Presentation

Lesson Time: 50 minutes

Lesson Objectives

In this lesson, you will secure and distribute a presentation. You will:

*   Secure a presentation

*   Broadcast a slide show

*   Create a video or a CD

Lesson Introduction

Not all presentations occur live in front of an audience, and for those that do, there are many reasons you may be asked to distribute or broadcast your presentation to a wider audience. Travel can be expensive, organizations can have members across the globe, and schedules often just don't mesh. You may need to use alternate channels for distributing your presentation to a large audience, not all of whom will always have PowerPoint available to them. And, once your presentation, and all of its information, is out there, you may become concerned about protecting your content.

PowerPoint 2010 offers a range of security and distribution options to help you deliver your presentation to everyone who needs to see it while keeping your content and information safe. Understanding how these various options work will give you the peace of mind that your content is secure and allow you to deliver a focused, effective presentation to people who were not able to attend the live event.

TOPIC A

Secure a Presentation

Information is a commodity. With the current capabilities of digital data storage and transfer, it is essential for organizations to keep a tight lid on sensitive information. Additionally, even minor changes to a presentation can alter the meaning of its content, and undo hours of hard work. When you need to share or distribute your presentations to a wide audience, you run the risk of exposing sensitive information or allowing your presentation to be edited, purposely or accidentally, by people who have no need to do so. Simply put, you will often need to secure your presentation to keep your information safe and your hard work intact.

PowerPoint 2010 contains a robust set of security options that allow you to determine exactly how secure your presentations need to be. You can control who has access to your presentations, and what, if anything, they can edit. You can also remove information you don't want shared and give recipients the assurance that a presentation has not been altered since you last worked on it.

Password Protection

Password Protection

Password protection allows you to secure your presentation files by requiring people to enter an alphanumeric sequence of characters to gain access to them. PowerPoint 2010 gives you the option of requiring a password on two different levels: whenever files are opened or in order for files to be modified.

The Mark as Final Feature

The Mark as Final Feature

The *Mark as Final feature* allows you to protect your presentation from changes once you have finished development. Enabling the **Mark as Final** feature converts the presentation file to a read-only state, discouraging other people from making changes to the file. When you launch a presentation that has been marked as final, a message is displayed below the tabs, and most ribbon commands are grayed out. You can access the **Mark as Final** feature by selecting **File→Info**, and then selecting the **Protect Presentation** button in the **Permissions** section.

 Note: It is possible for recipients to deactivate the **Mark as Final** feature. This feature only discourages editing; it does not prevent editing.

Digital Signatures

Digital Signatures

A *digital signature* is a virtual stamp that is used to authenticate digital content such as documents and email messages. Digital signatures are used to verify the identity of a sender and to ensure that no changes have been made to a document since it was signed. Digital signatures can be visible, meaning they appear within the actual document, or invisible. PowerPoint 2010 allows you to attach only an invisible digital signature to your documents.

PowerPoint documents with attached signatures display the **Signatures** pane, and an icon on the status bar when opened. The recipient must remove the digital signature to be able to edit the document. In order to add a digital signature to an Office 2010 document, you must have a valid digital ID.

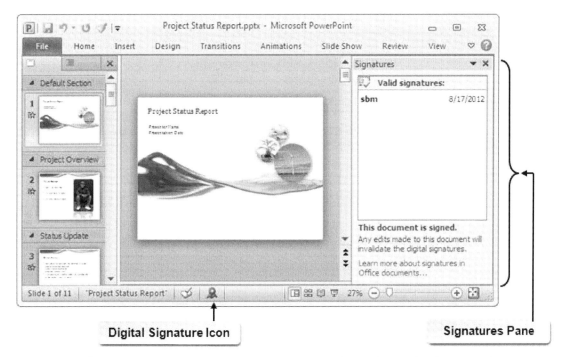

Digital Signature Icon

Signatures Pane

Figure 7-1: The Signatures pane and an icon on the status bar indicate the document has been digitally signed.

Digital IDs

Digital IDs, also known as digital certificates, make it possible to authenticate documents by using digital signatures. Digital IDs can be obtained through independent third-party organizations known as certificate authorities, or you can create your own. Digital certificates obtained through certificate authorities can be authenticated by anyone. If you create your own digital certificate, your digital signatures can be authenticated only from your computer.

Digital IDs

If you attempt to digitally sign a document and you don't have a digital ID, the **Get a Digital ID** dialog box is displayed, prompting you to decide how to obtain a digital certificate.

Get a Digital ID   [?] [X]

In order to sign a Microsoft Office document, you need a
digital ID. You have two options for getting a digital ID:

◉ **Get a digital ID from a Microsoft partner**

If you use a digital ID from a Microsoft partner, other people
will be able to verify the authenticity of your signature.

○ **Create your own digital ID**

If you create your own digital ID, other people will not be able
to verify the authenticity of your signature. You will be able
to verify the authenticity of your signature, but only on this
computer.

Learn more about digital   [OK]   [Cancel]
IDs in Office...

Figure 7–2: The Get a Digital ID dialog box.

The Trust Center Dialog Box

The Trust Center Dialog
Box

The **Trust Center** dialog box provides you with access to a number of options for configuring
security settings for your PowerPoint documents. The **Trust Center** dialog box displays tabbed
categories for which you can modify permissions and privacy settings.

> **Note:** Microsoft recommends consulting your system administrator before changing Trust
> Center settings. You can access more information on the Trust Center at Office.microsoft.com.

Trust Center Dialog Box Tab	Is Used To
Trusted Publishers	View and manage a list of software coders whose macros, add-ins, and other content you trust. Content from trusted publishers will always open.
Trusted Locations	Assign folders on your computer to be used to store files from trusted sources. Files stored in a trusted location are not subject to file validation.
Trusted Documents	Set options for how Office applications interact with active content, such as macro-enabled presentations.
Add-ins	Determine whether or not to require add-ins to contain a signature from the publisher, and whether or not to disable all add-ins.
ActiveX Settings	Select what prompts to display for ActiveX controls.
Macro Settings	Enable or disable macros and macro notifications.
Protected View	Determine which types of sources will open presentations in **Protected** view.
Message Bar	Enable or disable the message bar for active content.
File Block Settings	Determine which file types PowerPoint will block from opening or saving.

Trust Center Dialog Box Tab	Is Used To
Privacy Options	Enable or disable various privacy options for Office applications.

The Document Inspector Dialog Box

Before publicly sharing your presentations, you may wish to inspect your document for any hidden information that you might not want included in the document. The **Document Inspector** dialog box allows you to search your presentation for hidden information, and select any you wish to remove. You can access the **Document Inspector** dialog box by selecting **File→Info** and then selecting **Check for Issues** in the **Prepare for Sharing** section.

PowerPoint presentations can contain a number of types of personal and hidden information.

The Document Inspector Dialog Box

Information Type	Description
Comments and Annotations	Remarks left by reviews or collaborators, which can contain the names of people who worked on the project and reveal information about changes made throughout the development process.
Document Properties and Personal Information	Metadata that can include the name of the author, the subject and title of the presentation, the name of the person who most recently saved the presentation, the date the document was created, and file path information.
Custom XML Data	XML data that is not visible in the presentation.
Invisible On-Slide Content	Objects that have been formatted to be invisible, but still exist on the slides.
Off-Slide Content	Objects that have been dragged off of the visible portion of the slide.
Presentation Notes	The speaker notes authored in the **Notes** pane. There may be information in the notes intended only for the presenter. You may not wish to share this information with a wide audience.

Ask students about what types of hidden information they may have inadvertently left in presentations. Have they ever simply placed a graphic over something rather than delete it?

Note: To further explore hidden information, you can access the LearnTO **Keep Sensitive Information Out of Your Presentations** presentation from the **LearnTO** tile on the LogicalCHOICE Course screen.

Access the Checklist tile on your LogicalCHOICE course screen for reference information and job aids on How to Secure a Presentation

You may want to show LearnTO **Keep Sensitive Information Out of Your Presentations** from the LogicalCHOICE Course screen or have students navigate out to the Course screen and watch it themselves as a supplement to your instruction. If not, please remind students to visit the LearnTOs for this course on their LogicalCHOICE Course screen after class for supplemental information and additional resources.

ACTIVITY 7-1
Securing a Presentation

Data File

C:\091032Data\Securing and Distributing a Presentation\Develetech New Products Launch.pptx

Scenario

You are ready to send out the New Product Launch communication to the entire company. But because not everyone outside the company is privy to the new product information yet, you decide to use some of PowerPoint 2010's security features to keep information from leaking to the wrong people. You want to add password protection to the presentation, with the intention of emailing the password to audience members in a separate message, and you decide to mark the presentation as final to discourage people from making unapproved changes to the presentation once it begins to circulate.

1. Launch the C:\091032Data\Securing and Distributing a Presentation\Develetech New Products Launch.pptx file.

2. Save the presentation to the C:\091032Data\Securing and Distributing a Presentation folder as *My_Develetech New Products Launch.pptx*.

3. Require a password to view the presentation.

   a) Select **File→Save As** and, in the **Save As** dialog box, select **Tools** Tools ▼ .
   b) Select **General Options** from the drop-down menu.
   c) In the **General Options** dialog box, enter a password in the **Password to open** field, and then select **OK**.
   d) Make a note of your password.
   e) In the **Confirm Password** dialog box, re-enter the password, and then select **OK**.
   f) Select **Save** and select **Yes** to replace the file.

4. Mark the presentation as final.
   a) Select **File→Info**, and then select **Protect Presentation** in the **Permissions** section.
   b) Select **Mark as Final** in the drop-down menu and, in the **Microsoft PowerPoint** dialog box, select OK.

    Note: Marking the presentation as final automatically saves the presentation, which will overwrite the original data file. If you wish to go back and perform this activity again, and you have overwritten the data file or forgotten your password, a clean version of the Develetech New Products Launch.pptx file has been provided in the C:\091032Data\Securing and Distributing a Presentation\Clean File folder.

   c) In the subsequent **Microsoft PowerPoint** dialog box, select OK.

5. Verify your changes.
   a) Select **Home** and verify that the **Marked as Final** message appears.
   b) Close and re-open the file.
   c) Enter your password and select OK.

TOPIC B

Broadcast a Slide Show

Distance can be one of the greatest challenges when it comes to getting event participants in the same room at the same time. With so many organizations reaching globally, partnering with other organizations around the world, it is becoming increasingly necessary to hold live events with participants from a wide variety of locales.

PowerPoint 2010 gives you the ability to broadcast your presentations live via the web. Developing the skills necessary to run a live broadcast of your presentations provides you with massive reach when it comes to bringing colleagues from across the globe together at the same time at little to no cost.

The Broadcast Slide Show Option

The *Broadcast Slide Show option* allows you to share your presentations over the web, in real time, to anyone with Internet access and a web browser. You can also run a broadcast across an internal network to anyone within your organization who has network access. You can access the **Broadcast Slide Show** option by selecting **File→Save & Send**, and then selecting **Broadcast Slide Show** from the **Save & Send** section.

The Broadcast Slide Show Option

 Note: There is no audio support in PowerPoint 2010 for broadcasting presentations over the web. You will have to use an alternate audio system, such as phone conferencing, for the presenter and the audience to be able to hear each other.

The PowerPoint Broadcast Service

The *PowerPoint Broadcast Service* is a free service available to anyone with a Windows Live ID that allows you to broadcast your presentations across the web. The PowerPoint Broadcast Service generates a URL that you can send to participants so they can link to the broadcast. Although the presenter will have to sign in with a Windows Live ID, there are no sign-in requirements for audience members.

The Broadcast Slide Show Dialog Box

The Broadcast Slide Show dialog box provides you with commands to select a broadcast service and to begin broadcasting a slide show.

The Broadcast Slide Show Dialog Box

Broadcast Slide Show Dialog Box Element	Function
Broadcast Service Section	Displays the currently selected broadcast service. This will default to the last service you used.
Change Broadcast Service Button	Allows you to select an alternate broadcast service for your presentation.
Start Broadcast button	Begins broadcasting your slide show.
Cancel button	Cancels the broadcast.

Broadcast Differences

Broadcast slide show presentations do not behave exactly the same as live or recorded presentations. There are four differences your audience members will experience during presentation broadcasts.

Broadcast Differences

Presentational Element	What's Different
Transitions	All transitions will appear as fades from the audience perspective as you advance forward through the slides. If you go back to the previous slide, there is no transition.
Audio	Audio does not broadcast to the audience. You will need to set up a conference call or use another audio service for the presenter and the audience to hear each other.
Video	If you play video over a broadcast, the video will not be displayed in the audience member's browsers. PowerPoint broadcasts support hyperlink functionality, so, as an alternative, you can post the video to a web-based location and provide a hyperlink to the participants.
Annotation Tools	Annotation tools, such as the laser pointer and highlighter, will not be displayed to the audience.

 Note: You cannot edit slides during a broadcast. If you need to modify content on a slide, you will have to end the broadcast, make your changes, and then start a new broadcast.

Media File Compression

Some services maintain a file size limit for broadcasts, meaning it may be necessary to reduce the size of your presentation before starting a broadcast. PowerPoint 2010 provides you with a *media file compression* option that will reduce the size of media files, such as audio and video, thus decreasing the overall size of your presentation.

 Access the Checklist tile on your LogicalCHOICE course screen for reference information and job aids on How to Broadcast a Slide Show

ACTIVITY 7-2
Broadcasting a Slide Show

Before You Begin

Pair up with a partner for the activity. One of you will play the role of the communications director and the other will play the role of the sales manager.

You have a Windows Live ID.

Note: Make sure you have access to your Microsoft Live ID login credentials.

Note: If you are using a Windows Live ID that you created or that your instructor created for you solely for the purposes of this course, you may wish to delete the account when you are finished taking the course. To deactivate a Windows account, go to https://login.live.com/, log in using your credentials, select **Close account** from the bottom of the **Account summary** page, and follow the prompts.

If you have an odd number of students, you can participate in this activity. Also, if time permits, students can perform the activity twice, switching roles for each turn.

Scenario

One of Develetech's sales managers wants to discuss the custom slide show you (the communications director) created for the sales reps. You have a scheduled call to discuss other matters regarding the new product launch, and so you decide to broadcast the presentation via the web, so the sales manager can go over the presentation with you in real time. To facilitate a smooth broadcast, you decide to compress your media files before broadcasting. Because you have already marked the presentation as final, you will have to enable editing before you can compress the files.

---

1. Both: In the **Marked as Final** message along the top of the screen, select **Edit Anyway**.

2. Both: Compress the media files.
   a) Select **File→Info** and, in the **Media Size and Performance** section, select **Compress Media**.
   b) Select **Internet Quality** from the drop-down menu.
   c) When the file compression is complete, select **Close**.

Remote students are encouraged to use the private chat feature in their web conferencing tool to communicate with their partners to avoid clutter on the audio feed.

3. Communications director: Prepare to broadcast the presentation.
   a) Select **Save & Send** from the **Backstage** view and, from the **Save & Send** section, select **Broadcast Slide Show**.
   b) Select **Broadcast Slide Show** from the right pane.
   c) In the **Broadcast Slide Show** dialog box, ensure that **PowerPoint Broadcast Service** is displayed in the **Broadcast Service** section.
   d) Select **Start Broadcast**.
   e) If prompted, enter your Windows Live ID credentials, and then select **OK**.
   f) Select **Copy Link**, and then either email, chat, or instant message the link to your partner.

4. Sales manager: Access the broadcast by clicking the link or copying and pasting it into your web browser.

5. Communications director: Broadcast the presentation.
   a) In the **Broadcast Slide Show** dialog box, select **Start Slide Show**.
   b) Allow the slide show to play out, or navigate the slide show by using the action buttons.

6. Communications director: End the slide show and the broadcast.
   a) Press the **Esc** key to exit the slide show.
   b) In the **Broadcast View** message along the top of the screen, select **End Broadcast**.
   c) In the **Microsoft PowerPoint** dialog box, select **End Broadcast**.

7. Sales manager: Close the web browser tab displaying the presentation.

8. Time permitting, switch roles, and then repeat the activity from step 3.

TOPIC C

Create a Video or a CD

Distance may not always be your greatest obstacle when it comes to bringing event participants together. The modern work schedule has become so tight, your calendar and those of your audience members can often look like a solid block of commitments. It is simply not always possible to bring people together at the same time. You may need a way to distribute your presentation to people in a format that allows them to "attend" according to their schedules.

PowerPoint 2010 offers you several options for converting your presentations into video files and packaging them as physical discs. The ability to create presentations in these various formats allows you to deliver your message to anyone, anywhere in the world, at any time.

The Create a Video Option

The *Create a Video option* allows you to convert your presentation into a Windows Media Video (WMV)-formatted file that you can upload to the web, share via email, or transfer to others by using various "hard copy" methods such as thumb drives. You can access the **Create a Video** option by selecting **File→Save & Send**. The **Create a Video** section in the right pane allows you to configure various options before converting your presentation to a video file.

The Create a Video Option

 Note: You can also use third-party utilities to convert your presentations into alternate video file formats, such as .avi or .mov.

Create a Video Option	Function
Computer & HD Displays	Creates a high definition video, with an aspect ratio of 960 × 720, for use on computer monitors, projectors, or high-definition displays.
Internet & DVD	Creates a standard definition video, with an aspect ratio of 640 × 480, for uploading to the web or burning to a standard DVD.
Portable Devices	Creates a low-quality video, with an aspect ratio of 320 × 240, for use on mobile devices
Don't Use Recorded Timings and Narrations	Disregards timings and narrations in the presentation during file conversion. You can set the default timing for the video file with the **Seconds to spend on each slide** spin box.
Use Recorded Timings and Durations	Includes timings and narrations in the video file. For slides that do not contain timing, PowerPoint uses the default timing set in the **Seconds to spend on each slide** spin box.
Record Timings and Narrations	Launches the **Record Slide Show** dialog box, allowing you to record timings and narrations before converting the file to a video.

Create a Video Option	Function
Preview Timings and Narrations	Displays a preview of the presentation's timings and narrations.

 Access the Checklist tile on your LogicalCHOICE course screen for reference information and job aids on How to Convert a Presentation to a Video

ACTIVITY 7-3
Converting a Presentation to a Video

Scenario

During your meeting with the sales manager, she suggested you may want to save a copy of your presentation as a video and store it on the Develetech network. Then there would be an easily accessible copy of the information for people who delete or miss the email.

1. Convert the presentation to a video.
   a) Select **File→Save & Send→Create a Video**.
   b) In the **Create a Video** pane, ensure that **Computer and HD Displays** is selected in the first drop-down menu.
   c) Ensure that **Use Recorded Timings and Narrations** is selected in the second drop-down menu, and then select **Create Video**.

2. Save the video to the C:\091032Data\Securing and Distributing a Presentation folder as *My_Develetech New Products Launch.wmv*.

 Note: You can monitor the progress of the video creation on the status bar.

Converting the presentation to a video may take several minutes or longer. You may proceed with the lesson and subsequent activities while the conversion process runs in the background.

Ask the students why they might save the package to a folder instead of burning a CD right away. The answer may be as simple as they don't have access to a CD at the time. What are some other reasons?

The Package for CD Dialog Box

The Package Presentation for CD Option

The *Package Presentation for CD option* allows you to copy one or more PowerPoint presentations, along with any linked or embedded files or fonts, to a folder or directly to a CD. PowerPoint 2010 allows you to copy files to either CD-R or CD-RW discs. Audience members who do not have PowerPoint on their computers but who wish to view the presentation can download the PowerPoint Viewer. The CD package will include an HTML file with a link to download the viewer.

The Package for CD Dialog Box

The **Package for CD** dialog box allows you to configure your options for creating a CD package, and decide whether to copy your files to a CD or to a folder on your computer. You can access the **Package for CD** dialog box by selecting **File→Save & Send→Package Presentation for CD**, and then selecting **Package for CD** in the right pane.

Figure 7–3: The Package for CD dialog box.

Package for CD Dialog Box Option	Is Used To
Name the CD field	Enter a name for the packaged CD.
Files to Be Copied field	Display all of the presentation files to be included in the CD package, and to rearrange to order in which the files will appear. Linked or embedded files to be included in the package will not appear in this field, but will appear in the **PresentationPackage** folder within the final package.
Add button	Launch the **Add Files** dialog box, allowing you to add additional presentation files to the CD package.
Remove button	Remove presentation files from the CD package.
Copy to Folder button	Copy the files to a folder on your computer, as opposed to copying them directly to a CD.
Copy to CD button	Copy the files to a CD.
Options button	Launch the **Options** dialog box, allowing you to indicate which file types to include in the CD package, and to set password options.

 Access the Checklist tile on your LogicalCHOICE course screen for reference information and job aids on How to Package a Presentation as a CD

ACTIVITY 7-4

Packaging a Presentation

Scenario

Develetech archives all marketing and branding, and all communications presentations. You have already saved a copy of your presentation video to the network, but want to create a hard-copy backup just to be safe. You decide to package the presentation.

1. Prepare the presentation for packaging.
   a) Select **File→Save & Send→Package Presentation for CD**, and then select **Package for CD** in the right pane.
   b) In the **Package for CD** dialog box, in the **Name the CD** field, type *Prod Rel Bkup*.
   c) Select **Options**.
   d) In the **Options** dialog box, verify that the **Linked files** and the **Embedded TrueType** fonts check boxes are checked, and then select **OK**.

2. Save the package to a folder.
   a) Select **Copy to Folder**.
   b) In the **Copy to Folder** dialog box, select **Browse**, navigate to the C:\091032Data\Securing and Distributing a Presentation folder, and then select **Select**.
   c) Uncheck the **Open folder when complete** check box.
   d) Select **OK**.
   e) In the **Microsoft PowerPoint** dialog box, select **Yes**.
   f) If necessary, in the subsequent **Microsoft PowerPoint** dialog box, select **Continue**.
   g) In the **Package for CD** dialog box, select **Close**.

3. Save the presentation, and then close PowerPoint 2010.

Summary

You have secured your presentation, prepared it for distribution, and made video and CD package copies to archive your content for future use. Taking advantage of the security and distribution features in PowerPoint 2010 provides you with the ability to deliver your message and keep your content secure in nearly any situation. You have a variety of options for storing your content so that you can revisit and reference it long after you switch computers or jobs.

How likely are you to use PowerPoint to present confidential information now that you are aware of the security features available?

A: Answers will vary, but will likely depend on the nature of the content, the logistics of sharing passwords with other people, and the cost effectiveness of purchasing digital IDs.

Do you think the ability to broadcast presentations over the web will lead to a decrease in the number of live presentations? Do you prefer a live event over attending remotely?

A: Answers will vary depending on the job role and the personality of the audience member, and the type of organization for which he or she works. Although web communications will likely increase the number of overall presentations people are able to attend, it is not likely that live events will decrease significantly any time soon.

 Note: Check your LogicalCHOICE Course screen for opportunities to interact with your classmates, peers, and the larger LogicalCHOICE online community about the topics covered in this course or other topics you are interested in. From the Course screen you can also access available resources for a more continuous learning experience.

 Note: While you may not always be able to present live at an event, often times you will be. To explore methods for delivering engaging presentations, you can access the LearnTO **Effectively Deliver Presentations** presentation from the **LearnTO** tile on the LogicalCHOICE Course screen.

Encourage remote students to respond via chat or the video feed if it's available. The second question is particularly relevant to those participating in the class remotely.

Encourage students to use the social networking tools provided on the LogicalCHOICE Home screen to follow up with their peers after the course is completed for further discussion and resources to support continued learning.

You may want to show LearnTO **Effectively Deliver Presentations** from the LogicalCHOICE Course screen or have students navigate out to the Course screen and watch it themselves as a supplement to your instruction. If not, please remind students to visit the LearnTOs for this course on their LogicalCHOICE Course screen after class for supplemental information and additional resources.

Course Follow-Up

Congratulations! You have completed the *Microsoft® Office PowerPoint® 2010: Part 2* course. You have created a complex, diverse, engaging presentation, using a customized environment, that you can securely deliver to a wide audience via a number of delivery channels.

It is unlikely that the demand for multimedia presentation will wane any time soon. In fact, you are likely to be called upon to deliver messages more often, and in a wider variety of situations. Whatever the message, and whatever the situation, you can be confident in your ability to use PowerPoint 2010 to your advantage. Use the tools and the capabilities within PowerPoint to make your presentations stand out from the crowd, adapt to meet any situational requirements, and keep your confidential information safe.

What's Next?

Although there is no formal follow-up to the *Microsoft Office PowerPoint 2010: Part 2* course, you are encouraged to continue exploring the PowerPoint 2010 application to take full advantage of its robust capabilities. There are numerous educational resources available on the **office.microsoft.com** website. Logical Operations encourages you to explore PowerPoint further by actively participating in any of the social media forums set up by your instructor or training administrator through the **Social Media** tile on the LogicalCHOICE Course screen.

A | Microsoft Office PowerPoint 2010 Exam 77–883

Selected Logical Operations courseware addresses Microsoft Office Specialist (MOS) certification skills for Microsoft Office 2010. The following table indicates where PowerPoint 2010 skills that are tested on Exam 77-883 are covered in the Logical Operations Microsoft Office PowerPoint 2010 series of courses.

Objective Domain	Covered In
1. Managing the PowerPoint Environment	
1.1 Adjust views	
1.1.1 Adjust views using the ribbon	Part 1
1.1.2 Adjust views by status bar commands	Part 1
1.2 Manipulate the PowerPoint window	
1.2.1 Work with multiple presentation windows simultaneously	Part 2, Topic 1-A
1.3 Configure the Quick Access toolbar	
1.3.1 Show the QAT below the ribbon	Part 2, Topic 1-A
1.4 Configure the PPT file options	
1.4.1 Use PPT proofing	Part 1
1.4.2 Use PPT save options	Part 1
2. Creating a Slide Presentation	
2.1 Construct and edit photo albums	
2.1.1 Add captions to picture	Part 1
2.1.2 Insert text	Part 1
2.1.3 Insert images in black and white	Part 1
2.1.4 Reorder pictures in an album	Part 1
2.1.5 Adjust image	Part 1
2.1.5.1 Rotation	Part 1
2.1.5.2 Brightness	Part 1
2.1.5.3 Contrast	Part 1

Objective Domain	Covered In
2.2 Apply slide size and orientation settings	
2.2.1 Set up a custom size	Part 1
2.2.2 Change the orientation	Part 1
2.3 Add and remove slides	
2.3.1 Insert an outline	Part 1
2.3.2 Reuse slides from a saved presentation	Part 1
2.3.3 Reuse slides from a slides library	Part 2, Topic 5-B
2.3.4 Duplicate selected slides	Part 1
2.3.5 Duplicate multiple slides simultaneously	Part 1
2.3.6 Include noncontiguous slides in a presentation	Part 1
2.4 Format slides	
2.4.1 Format sections	Part 2, Topic 5-A
2.4.2 Modify themes	Part 1
2.4.3 Switch to a different slide layout	Part 1
2.4.4 Apply formatting to a slide	
2.4.4.1 Fill color	Part 1
2.4.4.2 Gradient	Part 1
2.4.4.3 Picture	Part 1
2.4.4.4 Texture	Part 1
2.4.4.5 Pattern	Part 1
2.4.5 Set up slide footers	Part 2, Topic 2-B
2.5 Enter and format text	
2.5.1 use text effects	Part 1
2.5.2 Change text format	
2.5.2.1 Indentation	Part 1
2.5.2.2 Alignment	Part 1
2.5.2.3 Line spacing	Part 1
2.5.2.4 Direction	Part 1
2.5.3 Change the formatting of bulleted and numbered lists	Part 1
2.5.4 Enter text in a placeholder text box	Part 1
2.5.5 Convert text to SmartArt	Part 2, Topic 3-A
2.5.6 Copy and paste text	Part 1
2.5.7 Use paste special	Part 1
2.5.8 Use format painter	Part 1
2.6 Format text boxes	
2.6.1 Apply formatting to a text box	

Objective Domain	Covered In
2.6.1.1 Fill color	Part 1
2.6.1.2 Gradient	Part 1
2.6.1.3 Picture	Part 1
2.6.1.4 Texture	Part 1
2.6.1.5 Pattern	Part 1
2.6.2 Change the outline of a text box	
2.6.2.1 Color	Part 1
2.6.2.2 Weight	Part 1
2.6.2.3 Style	Part 1
2.6.3 Change the shape of a text box	Part 1
2.6.4 Apply effects	Part 1
2.6.5 Set the alignment	Part 1
2.6.6 Create columns in a text box	Part 1
2.6.7 Set internal margins	Part 1
2.6.8 Set the current text box formatting as the default for new text boxes	Part 1
2.6.9 Adjust text in a text box	
2.6.9.1 Wrap	Part 1
2.6.9.2 Size	Part 1
2.6.9.3 Position	Part 1
2.6.10 Use auto-fit	Part 1
3. Working with Graphical and Multimedia Elements	
3.1 Manipulate graphical elements	
3.1.1 Arrange graphical elements	Part 1
3.1.2 Position graphical elements	Part 1
3.1.3 Resize graphical elements	Part 1
3.1.4 Apply effects to graphical elements	Part 1
3.1.5 Apply styles to graphical elements	Part 1
3.1.6 Apply borders to graphical elements	Part 1
3.1.7 Apply hyperlinks to graphical elements	Part 2, Topic 6-D
3.2 Manipulate images	
3.2.1 Apply color adjustments	Part 1
3.2.2 Apply image corrections	
3.2.2.1 Sharpen	Part 1
3.2.2.2 Soften	Part 1
3.2.2.3 Brightness	Part 1
3.2.2.4 Contrast	Part 1

Objective Domain	Covered In
3.2.3 Add artistic effects to an image	Part 1
3.2.4 Remove a background	Part 1
3.2.5 Crop a picture	Part 1
3.2.6 Compress selected pictures/all pictures	Part 1
3.2.7 Change a picture	Part 1
3.2.8 Reset a picture	Part 1
3.3 Modify WordArt and shapes	
3.3.1 Set the formatting of the current shape as the default for future shapes	Part 1
3.3.2 Change the fill color or texture	Part 1
3.3.3 Change the WordArt	Part 1
3.3.4 Convert WordArt to SmartArt	Part 2, Topic 3-A
3.4 Manipulate SmartArt	
3.4.1 Add and remove shapes	Part 1
3.4.2 Change SmartArt styles	Part 2, Topic 3-B
3.4.3 Change the SmartArt layout	Part 2, Topic 3-B
3.4.4 Reorder shapes	Part 2, Topic 3-B
3.4.5 Convert a SmartArt graphic to text	Part 2, Topic 3-B
3.4.6 Convert SmartArt to shapes	Part 2, Topic 3-B
3.4.7 Make shapes larger or smaller	Part 2, Topic 3-B
3.4.8 Promote bullet levels	Part 2, Topic 3-B
3.4.9 Demote bullet levels	Part 2, Topic 3-B
3.5 Edit video and audio content	
3.5.1 Apply a style to video or audio content	Part 2, Topics 4-A, 4-B
3.5.2 Adjust video or audio content	Part 2, Topics 4-A, 4-B
3.5.3 Arrange video or audio content	Part 2, Topic 4-B
3.5.4 Size video or audio content	Part 2, Topics 4-A, 4-B
3.5.5 Adjust playback options	Part 2, Topics 4-A, 4-B
4. Creating Charts and Tables	
4.1 Construct and modify tables	
4.1.1 Draw a table	Part 1
4.1.2 Insert a Microsoft Excel spreadsheet	Part 1
4.1.3 Set table and style options	Part 1
4.1.4 Add shading	Part 1
4.1.5 Add borders	Part 1
4.1.6 Add effects	Part 1
4.1.7 Columns and rows	

Objective Domain	Covered In
4.1.7.1 Change the alignment	Part 1
4.1.7.2 Resize	Part 1
4.1.7.3 Merge	Part 1
4.1.7.4 Split	Part 1
4.1.7.5 Distribute	Part 1
4.1.7.6 Arrange	Part 1
4.2 Insert and modify charts	
4.2.1 Select a chart type	Part 1
4.2.2 Enter chart data	Part 1
4.2.3 Change the chart type	Part 1
4.2.4 Change the chart layout	Part 1
4.2.5 Switch row and column	Part 1
4.2.6 Select data	Part 1
4.2.7 Edit data	Part 1
4.3 Apply chart elements	
4.3.1 Use chart labels	Part 1
4.3.2 Use axes	Part 1
4.3.3 Use gridlines	Part 1
4.3.4 Use backgrounds	Part 1
4.4 Manipulate chart layouts	
4.4.1 Select chart elements	Part 1
4.4.2 Format selections	Part 1
4.5 Manipulate chart elements	
4.5.1 Arrange chart elements	Part 1
4.5.2 Specify a precise position	Part 1
4.5.3 Apply effects	Part 1
4.5.4 Resize chart elements	Part 1
4.5.5 Apply quick styles	Part 1
4.5.6 Apply a border	Part 1
4.5.7 Add hyperlinks	Part 2, Topic 6-D
5. Applying Transitions and Animations	
5.1 Apply built-in and custom animations	
5.1.1 Use more entrance	Part 2, Topic 4-C
5.1.2 Use more emphasis	Part 2, Topic 4-C
5.1.3 Use more exit effects	Part 2, Topic 4-C
5.1.4 Use more motion paths	Part 2, Topic 4-C

Objective Domain	Covered In
5.2 Apply effect and path options	
5.2.1 Set timing	Part 2, Topic 4-C
5.2.2 Set start options	Part 2, Topic 4-C
5.3 Manipulate animations	
5.3.1 Change the direction of animations	Part 1
5.3.2 Attach a sound to an animation	Part 2, Topic 4-C
5.3.3 Use Animation Painter	Part 1
5.3.4 Reorder animation	Part 2, Topic 4-C
5.3.5 Select text options	Part 2, Topic 4-C
5.4 Apply and modify transitions between slides	
5.4.1 Modify a transition effect	Part 1
5.4.2 Add a sound to a transition	Part 1
5.4.3 Modify transition duration	Part 1
5.4.4 Set up manual or automatically timed advance options	Part 2, Topic 4-C
6. Collaborating on Presentations	
6.1 Manage comments in presentations	
6.1.1 Insert and edit comments	Part 2, Topic 5-A
6.1.2 Show or hide markup	Part 2, Topic 5-A
6.1.3 Move to the previous or next comment	Part 2, Topic 5-A
6.1.4 Delete comments	Part 2, Topic 5-A
6.2 Apply proofing tools	
6.2.1 Use spelling and thesaurus features	Part 1
6.2.2 Compare and combine presentations	Part 2, Topic 5-A
7. Preparing Presentations for Delivery	
7.1 Save presentations	
7.1.1 Save the presentation as a picture	Part 1
7.1.2 Save the presentation as a PDF	Part 1
7.1.3 Save the presentation as an XPS	Part 1
7.1.4 Save the presentation as an outline	Part 1
7.1.5 Save the presentation an open document	Part 1
7.1.6 Save the presentation as a show (.ppsx)	Part 1
7.1.7 Save a slide or object as a picture file	Part 1
7.2 Share presentations	
7.2.1 Share a presentation for CD delivery	Part 2, Topic 7-C
7.2.2 Create video	Part 2, Topic 7-C
7.2.3 Create handouts	Part 1

Objective Domain	Covered In
7.2.4 Compress media	Part 2, Topic 7-B
7.3 Print presentations	
7.3.1 Adjust print settings	Part 1
7.4 Protect presentations	
7.4.1 Set a password	Part 2, Topic 7-A
7.4.2 Change a password	Part 2, Topic 7-A
7.4.3 Mark a presentation as final	Part 2, Topic 7-A
8. Delivering Presentations	
8.1 Apply presentation tools	
8.1.1 Add pen and highlighter annotations	Part 2, Topic 6-A
8.1.2 Change the ink color	Part 2, Topic 6-A
8.1.3 Erase an annotation	Part 2, Topic 6-A
8.1.4 Discard annotations upon closing	Part 2, Topic 6-A
8.1.5 Retain annotations upon closing	Part 2, Topic 6-A
8.2 Set up slide shows	
8.2.1 Set up a slide show	Part 2, Topic 6-B
8.2.2 Play narrations	Part 2, Topic 6-B
8.2.3 Set up presenter view	Part 2, Topic 6-B
8.2.4 Use timings	Part 1
8.2.5 Show media controls	Part 2, Topic 4-A
8.2.6 Broadcast presentations	Part 2, Topic 7-B
8.2.7 Create a custom slide show	Part 2, Topic 6-C
8.3 Set presentation timing	
8.3.1 Rehearse timings	Part 2, Topic 6-E
8.3.2 Keep timings	Part 2, Topic 6-E
8.3.3 Adjust a slide's timing	Part 1
8.4 Record presentations	
8.4.1 Start recording from the beginning of slide show	Part 2, Topic 6-E
8.4.2 Start recording from the current slide of the slide show	Part 2, Topic 6-E

Microsoft PowerPoint 2010 Common Keyboard Shortcuts

The following table lists common keyboard shortcuts you can use in PowerPoint 2010.

Function	Shortcut
Change the font of selected text	Ctrl + Shift + F
Change the font size of selected text	Ctrl + Shift + P
Open the **Find** dialog box	Ctrl + F
Copy the selected text	Ctrl + C
Paste copied content	Ctrl + V
Select all	Ctrl + A
Undo the last action	Ctrl + Z
Apply or remove bold formatting	Ctrl + B
Apply or remove italic formatting	Ctrl + I
Apply or remove underline formatting	Ctrl + U
Insert a hyperlink	Ctrl + K
Center a paragraph	Ctrl + E
Justify a paragraph	Ctrl + J
Left align a paragraph	Ctrl + L
Right align a paragraph	Ctrl + R
Start a presentation from the beginning	F5
Advance to the next slide	N or Enter
Return to the previous slide	P or Backspace
Go to slide *number*	*number* + Enter
End a presentation	Esc
View the **All Slides** dialog box	Ctrl + S
Increase sound volume	Alt + Up
Decrease sound volume	Alt + Down

Lesson Labs

Lesson labs are provided for certain lessons as additional learning resources for this course. Lesson labs are developed for selected lessons within a course in cases when they seem most instructionally useful as well as technically feasible. In general, labs are supplemental, optional unguided practice and may or may not be performed as part of the classroom activities. Your instructor will consider setup requirements, classroom timing, and instructional needs to determine which labs are appropriate for you to perform, and at what point during the class. If you do not perform the labs in class, your instructor can tell you if you can perform them independently as self-study, and if there are any special setup requirements.

Lesson Lab 1-1
Customizing PowerPoint 2010

Activity Time: 5 minutes

Scenario

You're a new business development specialist for a regional marketing company. As such, you often pitch marketing campaign ideas to potential new clients. You find yourself adding a lot of video and audio content to your PowerPoint presentations to make them more exciting. You don't like having to navigate the ribbon frequently to get to the insert audio and insert video commands. So, you decide to add the commands to the **Home** tab on the ribbon to make them more accessible. You will need to remove some existing commands from the **Home** tab to accommodate the change.

You also feel it's a good idea to make a few other changes to the PowerPoint environment because you're taking the time to customize the ribbon.

---

1. Launch PowerPoint 2010.

2. Remove the Editing group from the Home tab.

3. Create a new group on the Home tab, and then name it *Audio/Video*.

4. Add the **Audio from File, Clip Art Audio, Clip Art Video, Video from File,** and **Video from Web Site** commands to the **Audio/Video** group.

5. Set PowerPoint 2010 to save files in the PowerPoint Presentation 97-2003 (.ppt) file format.

6. Set the maximum number of undos to 50.

Lesson Lab 2-1
Customizing a Template

Activity Time: 10 minutes

Data Files

C:\091032Data\Customizing Design Templates\Training Presentation.pptx

C:\091032Data\Customizing Design Templates\delivery van.wmf

Scenario

You are a human resources specialist for a chain of flower shops that specializes in delivering extravagant arrangements anywhere in the world. You have been asked to create a training and orientation template for various departments within the company. You have a presentation you would like to use as a template, but it doesn't fit your company's branding guidelines, and you want to customize the template so that it's a bit different for each of the departments. You decide to begin by creating a template for the drivers in the shipping department.

1. Launch the C:\091032Data\Customizing Design Templates\Training Presentation.pptx file.

2. Apply the **Clarity** theme to the slide master.

3. Apply the C:\091032Data\Customizing Design Templates\delivery van.wmf file as a background image to all slide layouts, with the transparency set to **85%**.

4. Remove the footers from the title slide layout.

5. Add a new slide layout to the template, and name it *Org Chart*.

6. Move the title text placeholder to the bottom of the Org Chart layout.

7. Add a SmartArt graphic placeholder to the Org Chart layout that fills most of the layout above the title text placeholder.

8. Close the **Slide Master** view, and then remove slides 5, 6, and 7 from the presentation.

9. Insert an Org Chart slide after slide 4.

10. Set the default number of slides to print on handouts to **3**.

11. Save the presentation as a template to the C:\0910932Data\Customizing Design Templates folder as *My_Training Presentation_shipping.potx*.

12. Close the file.

Lesson Lab 3–1
Creating a SmartArt Graphic

Activity Time: 10 minutes

Data File

C:\091032Data\Adding SmartArt to a Presentation\Fiscal Year Restructuring Plan.pptx

Scenario

Your company's board of directors is considering implementing a restructuring plan in an effort to strengthen the company's finances. As the operations manager, you report directly to the VP of operations, who has been asked to propose a new organizational structure. Your boss has started developing a PowerPoint presentation to deliver to the board of directors. However, as he is less familiar with the organizational structure of the company below the executive management level, he has asked you to review and complete the organizational chart he has started. You decide you would first like to convert the text version of the org chart into a SmartArt graphic, so it will easier for you to view and arrange.

1. Launch the C:\091032Data\Adding SmartArt to a Presentation\Fiscal Year Restructuring Plan.pptx file, and then navigate to slide 3.

2. Convert the bullet list text to a SmartArt graphic by using the **Organization Chart** layout from the **Hierarchy** SmartArt category.

3. Apply the **Metallic Scene** style to the SmartArt graphic.

4. Add a SmartArt shape above the **Communications Director** and the **Director of Marketing**, and type *V.P. of Communications* in the shape.

5. Change the text for the Communications Director to *Director of Communications*.

6. Increase the size of the SmartArt shapes for the **VP of Communications** and the **Director of Communications** to accommodate the text.

7. Save the presentation to the C:\091032Data\Adding SmartArt to a Presentation folder as **My_Fiscal Year Restructuring Plan.pptx**.

Lesson Lab 4-1
Adding Audio and Animation to a Slide

Activity Time: 10 minutes

Data Files

C:\091032Data\Working with Media and Animations\store display.pptx

C:\091032Data\Working with Media and Animations\swing.wav

Scenario

You own a store that specializes in vintage toys and collectibles, and you are developing a presentation that you would like to display on in-store monitors and in the front window to grab the attention of potential customers. You have designed the first slide, which is meant to give people an idea of the kinds of items your store carries. You feel the static text and the lack of multimedia will not have the effect you're looking for. So, you decide to animate the text and add some music to make the initial slide more captivating.

---

1. Launch the C:\091032Data\Working with Media and Animations\store display.pptx file.

2. Insert the **swing.wav** file on the slide.

3. Set the swing.wav file to play across slides, and set its volume level as low.

4. Hide the audio controls and the icon during slide shows.

5. Add the **Checkerboard** entrance animation effect to the text box that contains the list of store items.

    | **Note:** Make sure you apply the animation effect to the text box, and not the text itself.

6. Set the animation effect to start **With Previous**.

7. Set the duration of the animation effect to 02.50 seconds.

8. Set the animation effect to sequence by paragraph.

9. Set the animation effect for each of the words in the list, except for "Toys," to start after the previous effect.

10. View the slide show to preview the animation effects and audio.

11. Save the file to the C:\091032Data\Working with Media and Animations folder as *My_store display.pptx*.

12. Close the file.

Lesson Lab 5-1
Comparing Presentations and Storing Files Online

Activity Time: 15 minutes

Data Files

C:\091032Data\Collaborating on a Presentation\Video Production 101.pptx

C:\091032Data\Collaborating on a Presentation\Video Production 101_revised.pptx

Before You Begin

You have a Windows Live ID and a Windows Live SkyDrive account.

 Note: Have your login credentials available before beginning the lab.

Scenario

You are the new instructor for the introductory video production class at an art and film school. You have just finished developing the course curriculum for the fall semester. To introduce each unit of instruction, you decided to create brief PowerPoint presentations as an overview for the students. Your department chair asked to review your overview for the first unit before classes begin. You emailed her a copy of the presentation, and have just received her feedback in the form of a revised presentation. You use the Compare and Merge feature in PowerPoint 2010 to incorporate the feedback. Also, since you worked on the presentation from your office computer, you decide to store a copy of the file to your SkyDrive account so you can more easily develop the outline for future units from home.

1. Launch the C:\091032Data\Collaborating on a Presentation\Video Production 101.pptx file.

2. Use the Compare and Merge feature to open the Video Production_revised.pptx file.

3. Accept all of the changes in the presentation.

4. End the review and save your changes.

5. Save the file as *My_Video Production 101.pptx*.

6. Store the file My_Video Production 101.pptx to your SkyDrive account in the Documents folder.

7. Close the presentation.

Lesson Lab 6–1
Customizing a Slide Show

Activity Time: 10 minutes

Data File
C:\091032Data\Customizing a Slide Show\store display_final.pptx

Scenario
You are the owner of a vintage toy and collectibles store. You have finished creating a PowerPoint presentation that you want to run on monitors throughout your store and in the front window to promote your merchandise to potential customers. As you want it to run on a continuous loop, you set it up to run at a kiosk display, and to repeat after the final slide plays. You decide you would also like to add an engaging transition between slides to make the presentation more appealing.

---

1. Launch the C:\091032Data\Customizing a Slide Show\store display_final.pptx file.

2. Apply the **Gallery** slide transition to all slides in the presentation, and set the transition duration to 01.50 seconds.

3. Set all slide transitions to automatically advance after 01.00 second.

4. Set the slide show to be displayed at a kiosk, in a loop, while keeping slide timings.

5. Run the slide show.

6. End the slide show.

7. Save the presentation to the C:\091032Data\Customizing a Slide Show folder as *My_store display_final.pptx*.

8. Close the file.

Lesson Lab 7-1
Securing and Backing Up Your Presentation

Activity Time: 5 minutes

Data File
C:\091032\Securing and Distributing a Presentation\A Sound Investment.pptx

Scenario
You are meeting with a group of potential investors for your small chain of restaurants. You want to present financial information about your business to convince the investors that your company is a sound investment. You are meeting with the group at a neutral location, so you will have to travel with your presentation file. Because there is sensitive financial information in the presentation, you decide to password-protect the file and remove personal information. You also want to send the investors away with a hard copy of your presentation, so you decide to package the file to burn to a CD.

---

1. Launch the C:\091032\Securing and Distributing a Presentation\A Sound Investment.pptx file.

2. Require a password to open the file and to edit the file.

3. Package the presentation for CD as Invest Bkup in the C:\091032Data\Securing and Distributing a Presentation folder, ensuring that all linked files and embedded fonts save with the package.

4. Inspect the file for personal information before packaging.

5. Save the file to the C:\091032Data\Securing and Distributing a Presentation folder as *My_A Sound Investment.pptx*.

6. Close the file.

> **Note:** The only solution file provided for this lab is the folder for the CD package. Once password protection is set, the presentation file cannot be opened for inspection unless you have the password.

Glossary

action buttons
On-screen objects that are used to perform pre-defined functions.

annotation tools
A collection of tools used for marking PowerPoint slides during a slide show.

annotations
Markings that users can place on slides during a slide show to highlight key points or emphasize particular content.

Broadcast Slide Show option
Feature of PowerPoint 2010 that allows users to share a presentation in real time over the web.

co-authoring
Process by which multiple authors can simultaneously make changes to a single document that is stored on a server.

comments
Messages that reviewers can insert into the slides in a presentation without disturbing the slide content.

Create a Video option
Feature of PowerPoint 2010 that allows users to convert presentations into Windows Media Video (WMV)-formatted video files.

custom slide shows
Presentations that display only a selected sequence of slides.

custom themes
Definable combinations of colors, fonts, and effects that can be applied to the slides, slide layouts, and slide masters in PowerPoint.

digital IDs
Virtual certificates that make it possible to authenticate documents when using digital signatures.

digital signatures
Virtual stamps that are used to authenticate digital content, such as documents and email messages.

footers
Small content placeholders that can appear along the bottom of slides, handouts, and notes pages. These typically contain information such as the presenter's name, the presentation date, and page or slide numbers.

headers
Small content placeholders that can appear along the top of handouts and notes pages. These typically contain information such as the presenter's name and the presentation date.

hyperlinks
Navigational commands within documents or on web pages that are used to jump to other documents, other web pages, or another location within the current document or web page.

kiosks
Displays that are set up in public or high-traffic locations, such as trade shows, malls, or lobbies.

looping
The process of automatically replaying a slide show from the beginning, once the final slide has been displayed.

Mark as Final feature
Functionality contained in Microsoft Office applications that allows the creator of a document to discourage other users from making edits to the document once it is complete.

markup
Any visible changes or edits made to the content in a document.

media file compression
The process of reducing the size of digital files.

notes master
Element of PowerPoint 2010 that determines the placement, formatting, orientation, and styles of the content on notes pages.

Package Presentation for CD option
Feature of PowerPoint 2010 that allows users to copy one or more PowerPoint presentations, along with any linked or embedded files or fonts, to a folder or directly to a CD.

password protection
The process of securing a document by requiring other users to enter an alphanumeric sequence of characters in order to access or edit the document.

poster frames
The preview images that are displayed for videos in a presentation.

PowerPoint Broadcast Service
Free Microsoft service that allows PowerPoint 2010 users who have a Windows Live ID to broadcast presentations over the web.

PowerPoint Web App
Web-based version of PowerPoint that allows users to view and make edits to presentations that are saved to a SkyDrive account.

Presenter view
A mode of viewing PowerPoint presentations that provides different views of the slide show for the presenter and for the audience. This feature allows the presenter to perform particular tasks within the slide show without affecting the audience's experience.

Rehearse Timings feature
PowerPoint 2010 function that allows a presenter to automatically time slides when practicing the delivery of a presentation.

Revisions pane
Element of the PowerPoint 2010 user interface that allows users to compare two presentations and merge particular elements of the presentations.

Save to Web option
PowerPoint 2010 option that allows users to save presentations online by using a Windows Live ID.

Selection and Visibility pane
An element of the PowerPoint 2010 user interface that allows users to view the order in which objects appear on slides and rearrange on-slide objects.

slide library
A server-based repository for PowerPoint slides that allows for the sharing, versioning, editing, and updating of the slides stored in it.

slide masters
Elements of all PowerPoint 2010 presentations that determine the layout and thematic characteristics of the presentation's slides.

SmartArt graphics
Visual representations of textual content that typically represent a process, a cycle, a hierarchy, or relationships.

Windows Live SkyDrive
A server-based file storage service that allows users to upload, share, and set permissions for various file types.

Index

A

action buttons *89*
Action Settings dialog box *89*
Advanced options *10*
animation *53*
Animation pane *52*
annotation tools *78*
Arrow annotation tool *79*
audio
    controls *42*
    file formats *42*
Audio Tools contextual tab
    Playback tab *43*

B

bookmarks *43*
Broadcast Slide Show dialog box *103*

C

co-authoring a presentation *63*
comments *61*
Compare group *64*
contextual tabs
    Audio Tools *43*
    SmartArt Tools *36*
    Video Tools *47*
Create a Video option *107*
creating a slide layout *19*
custom
    themes *19*
customizing the ribbon *3*
Custom Shows dialog box *85*
custom slide show *85*

D

Define Custom Show dialog box *85*
digital IDs *99*
digital signature *98*
Document Inspector dialog box *101*

E

Edit in Browser feature *71*
editing
    presentations *62*, *64*
    video *49*
Effect Options dialog box *53*

F

file formats
    audio *42*
    video *47*
footers *22*
Format tab
    video commands *48*

H

handout master *27*
headers *22*
Highlighter annotation tool *79*
hyperlinks *88*

I

Insert Hyperlink dialog box *88*

K

kiosks *82*

L

looping *82*

M

managing slide content *37*
Mark as Final feature *98*
markup *62*
media file compression *104*

N

notes master *26*

P

Package for CD dialog box *109*
Package Presentation for CD option *109*
password protection *98*
Pen annotation tool *79*
Playback tab *43, 49*
poster frames *48*
PowerPoint Broadcast Service *103*
PowerPoint Options dialog box *3*
Presenter view *81*
publishing slides *69*

R

recording presentations *92*
Recording shortcut menu *92*
Record Slide Show dialog box *92*
Rehearse Timings feature *93*
Revisions pane *64*
ribbon
    customizing *3, 5*

S

Save options *10*
Save to Web option *71*
sections
    adding and managing *60*
Selection and Visibility pane *37*
Set Up Show dialog box *82*
SharePoint 2010 *68*
SkyDrive *71*
slide layouts
    creating *19*
slide library
    publishing slides to *69*
slide masters

commands *17*
slide shows
    broadcasting *103*
    custom *85*
    differences between broadcasting and
    recording *103*
    hidden information *101*
    password protection *98*
    recording *92*
    setting up *82*
    timing *93*
    video *107*
SmartArt graphics
    categories *33*
    designing *36*
    formatting *36*
    working with text *33*
status bar
    customizing *5*

T

Text pane *33*
Themes gallery *19*
Timing group *55*
timing slide shows *93*
Transitions tab *55*
Trim Audio dialog box *44*
Trust Center dialog box *100*

U

user interface *2*

V

video
    controls *42*
    editing *49*
    file formats *47*
Video Tools Contextual tab *47*

W

Web App *71*
Window group
    commands *8*
Windows Live SkyDrive *71*